Kitchen Design

Küchen Design

Design de cuisines

Diseño de cocinas

teNeues

Editor in chief:	Paco Asensio
Texts:	Marina Ubach
Editorial coordination:	Cynthia Reschke
Editorial assistant:	Simone K. Schleifer
Art director:	Mireia Casanovas Soley
Layout:	Ignasi Gracia Blanco
Copy-editing:	Francesc Bombí-Vilaseca, Haike Falkenberg
German translation:	Sven Mettner, Oliver Herzig
French translation:	Catherine Reschke
English translation:	Booksfactory *Translations*

Produced by Loft Publications
www.loftpublications.com

Published by teNeues Publishing Group

teNeues Publishing Company
16 West 22nd Street, New York, NY 10010, USA
Tel.: 001-212-627-9090, Fax: 001-212-627-9511

teNeues Book Division
Kaistraße 18
40221 Düsseldorf, Germany
Tel.: 0049-(0)211-994597-0, Fax: 0049-(0)211-994597-40

teNeues Publishing UK Ltd.
P.O. Box 402
West Byfleet
KT14 7ZF, Great Britain
Tel.: 0044-1932-403509, Fax: 0044-1932-403514

teNeues France S.A.R.L.
4, rue de Valence
75005 Paris, France
Tel.: 0033-1-55 76 62 05, Fax: 0033-1-55 76 64 19

teNeues Iberica S.L.
Pso. Juan de la Encina 2–48, Urb. Club de Campo
28700 S.S.R.R., Madrid, Spain
Tel./Fax: 0034-91-65 95 876

www.teneues.com

ISBN-10:	3-8238-4522-5
ISBN-13:	978-3-8238-4522-5

© 2005 teNeues Verlag GmbH + Co. KG, Kempen

Printed in Spain

Bibliographic information published by Die Deutsche Bibliothek. Die Deutsche Bibliothek lists this publication in the Deutsche Nationalbibliografie; detailed bibliographic data is available in the Internet at http://dnb.ddb.de.

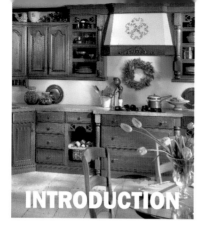

INTRODUCTION

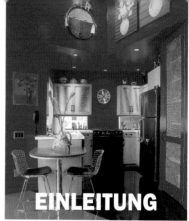

EINLEITUNG

The concept of the kitchen has evolved with time. At the outset of the twentieth century, it was a forgotten room, relegated to a secondary place and never revealed to society. Even in some more humble homes, the kitchen was a place exclusively for cooks and servants. All that mattered was the final product of the activity that took place within: the meals to be served in the dining room. As such, the distribution and appearance of the room were unimportant. Yet, as servants gradually disappeared from the home, women were forced to assume all of their previous responsibilities. At the same time, the location of the kitchen remained in the most isolated part of the house. While domestic appliances were conceived with the objective of liberating women from the rigors of housework, in reality they only added to women's responsibilities. With technological advance also came more clothes to wash and more meals to cook. Women's place only began to change when women decided to distance themselves from purely domestic-oriented work and look for jobs outside of the home. With the passage

Das Konzept der Küche hat sich im Laufe der Zeit verändert. Zu Beginn des 20. Jahrhunderts spielte sie als Raum nur eine untergeordnete Rolle und wurde niemals öffentlich gezeigt. Es war ein Ort, der selbst in manch bescheidenem Haushalt nur den Köchen und dem Dienstpersonal vorbehalten war. Von Interesse war lediglich das Resultat der Arbeit, d. h. die Gerichte, die im Esszimmer serviert wurden, und es war vollkommen gleichgültig, wie die Küche eingerichtet war oder aussah. Nach und nach verschwand das Dienstpersonal aus den Haushalten und die Frau des Hauses war gezwungen dessen Stelle einzunehmen, und sich um sämtliche Aufgaben zu kümmern, während sich die Küche weiterhin im entlegensten Winkel des Hauses befand. Es wurden zwar Küchengeräte mit dem ausdrücklichen Ziel entwickelt, der Hausfrau die schweren häuslichen Arbeiten abzunehmen. In der Praxis hieß das jedoch, dass sie nur noch mehr Aktivitäten zu kontrollieren hatte: Die Neuerungen brachten es mit sich, dass mehr Wäsche zu waschen und mehr Essen zu kochen war. Die gesellschaftliche Stellung der

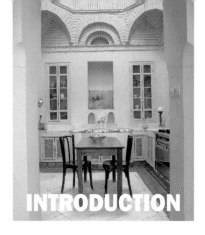

INTRODUCTION

INTRODUCCIÓN

Le concept de la cuisine a évolué avec le temps. Au début du 20ème siècle, c'était une pièce oubliée, reléguée à une place secondaire, jamais montrée en société. Même dans les demeures les plus humbles elle était réservée aux cuisiniers et aux serviteurs, uniquement intéressante pour le résultat final étant les repas servis dans la salle à manger. De ce fait l'agencement et l'apparence n'avaient guère d'importance. Peu à peu, les serviteurs disparaissant progressivement, les maîtresses de maison furent contraintes d'assumer leurs tâches. A cette époque la cuisine était encore située dans la partie la plus à l'écart de la maison. Les appareils ménagers destinés à libérer les femmes de certaines contraintes ménagères leur amenèrent en réalité de nouvelles responsabilités. Avec les progrès techniques, il y eût plus de lessive à laver et plus de repas à préparer. La place de la femme ne changea qu'au moment où elle décida de se distancer des tâches purement domestiques et de chercher du travail à l'extérieur. Avec les années et les nouvelles technologies, cette pièce est intégrée au reste de la maison et se

El concepto de cocina ha ido evolucionando con el paso del tiempo. A principios del siglo XX se trataba de una habitación olvidada, relegada a un segundo término, que nunca se mostraba en sociedad. La cocina era un lugar únicamente para cocineros y sirvientes, incluso en algunas viviendas humildes. Sólo interesaba por el resultado final de su actividad: por la elaboración de los guisos que se servían en el comedor, pero a nadie le importaba cómo se organizaba esta estancia y qué aspecto tenía. Poco a poco los sirvientes fueron desapareciendo de los hogares y la mujer tuvo que sustituirlos y ocuparse de todas las tareas, mientras esta habitación seguía ocupando la zona más aislada de la casa. Los aparatos domésticos nacieron con la intención de liberar a la mujer de las duras tareas del hogar, aunque, en la práctica, repercutieron en el aumento de las actividades que ella debía controlar: con los nuevos avances había más ropa que lavar y más comidas que guisar. El cambio de posición de la mujer surge cuando decide apartarse de las tareas puramente domésticas y buscar trabajo

of time as well as technological advance, the kitchen came to be more fully integrated into the rest of the house as a luminous and practical space.

The gradual disappearance of the dining room as the center of family reunion, coupled with the growing concern for comfort and technological advance, have converted the kitchen into the most important room in the house—the place where meals are prepared and the family gathers to be together. As the room where guests are received, today's kitchen fulfills the role of living rooms in the eighteenth and nineteenth centuries. As a result, it has become one of the most prominent rooms in the house. More time is invested than before in the selection of kitchen materials and decorations. Today's kitchens are larger and fitted out with multiple pragmatic solutions which increase capacity and level of

Frau veränderte sich erst, als sie sich nicht mehr nur allein der Hausarbeit widmete, sondern sich eine Beschäftigung außerhalb des Hauses suchte. Im Laufe der Jahre und dank des technischen Fortschritts verwandelte sich die Küche in einen hellen und praktischen Raum, der sich dem restlichen Haus öffnet.

Das allmähliche Verschwinden des Esszimmers als Mittelpunkt des Familienlebens sowie die wachsende Bedeutung von Bequemlichkeit und technischem Fortschritt machen die Küche von heute zum wichtigsten Bereich des Hauses: dem Ort, wo das Essen zubereitet wird und sich gleichzeitig die Familie trifft. Gegenwärtig spielt die Küche die Rolle eines Salons des 18. und 19. Jahrhunderts, in dem die Gäste empfangen wurden, und nimmt nunmehr im Haus einen zentralen Platz ein. Es wird mehr Zeit in die Auswahl ihrer Einrichtung und Ausstattung investiert, und zugleich erhält die Küche mehr Raum mit zahlreichen praktischen Lösungen, wodurch ihre Kapazität erhöht und sie besser durchorganisiert wird. Das Konzept der neuen Küche weist

transforme en un espace lumineux et pratique.

La disparition progressive de la salle à manger comme centre de réunion de la famille ajouté à une augmentation du confort et une technologie poussée, ont converti la cuisine actuelle en l'une des pièces les plus importante de la maison, l'endroit où les repas viennent préparés et où la famille se réunit. Aujourd'hui la cuisine prend la place que tenait le salon au 18ième et 19ième siècle, un endroit où l'on reçoit les visites. Elle est l'une des pièces les plus importante de la maison. On investit toujours plus de temps dans

fuera de la casa. Con el paso de los años y los nuevos avances tecnológicos, esta habitación se abre al resto de la casa para convertirse en un espacio luminoso y práctico.

La progresiva desaparición del comedor como centro de reunión de la familia y la mayor preocupación por la comodidad y los avances tecnológicos han convertido la cocina actual en la zona más importante de la casa, donde se preparan los alimentos y al mismo tiempo se reúne la familia. La cocina desempeña actualmente el papel de salón de los siglos XVIII y XIX, lugar donde se recibían las visitas de la casa, y en la actualidad es una de las habitaciones protagonistas de la vivienda. Se invierte mayor tiempo en la elección de los materiales y en su decoración, y se le adjudica mayor espacio y múltiples soluciones prácticas, para ampliar su capacidad y organización. El nuevo concepto de cocina distribuye

organization. The new concept for kitchens envisions particular areas for each activity; in such a way that the kitchen may be utilized comfortably while space is left for the family to come together at mealtime. New homes with an open multifunctional structure, however, opt for a different concept: open spaces without walls, with the kitchen open to the rest of the home and a versatile space for meals which, according to necessity, can be converted into a work table for both children and adults. All contemporary designs advocate comfortable, luminous spaces in which preparation of meals and sitting at table become genuine pleasures.

spezifischen Arbeiten ihre eigenen Bereiche zu, die dadurch bequem zu nutzen sind und Raum lassen, um beisammenzusitzen und zu essen. Moderne Wohnungen mit ihren offenen und multifunktionalen Strukturen setzen dem ein anderes Konzept entgegen: offene Räume ohne Trennwände mit einer Küche, die nicht mehr vom Rest des Hauses abgetrennt ist, sowie einen flexiblen Raum zum Essen, der sich ganz nach Bedarf in einen Arbeitsbereich für Kinder und Erwachsene verwandeln kann. Die aktuelle Architektur setzt auf bequeme und helle Räume, in denen es eine wahre Freude ist, das Essen zuzubereiten und am Tisch Platz zu nehmen.

le choix des matériaux et à sa décoration. On lui attribue une place plus grande et de nombreuses solutions pratiques en augmentent la capacité et l'organisation. Le nouveau concept de la cuisine prévoit des espaces particuliers à chaque activité. Ils peuvent être utilisés plus commodément tout en réservant une place pour se réunir et pour manger. Les habitations nouvelles avec leur structure ouverte et multifonctionnelle optent pour un concept différent : des espaces ouverts, sans parois, la cuisine ouverte sur le reste de la maison avec un espace polyvalent pour prendre les repas, avec une table pouvant être convertie, en cas de nécessité en une table de travail pour les enfants ou les adultes. Le design contemporain plaide pour des espaces confortables et lumineux, où préparer les repas et être assis à table deviennent un vrai plaisir.

cada uno de los trabajos en distintas áreas. De esta forma, cada una de las zonas puede utilizarse cómodamente y se reserva un espacio para la reunión y la comida. Las nuevas viviendas de estructura abierta y multifuncional apuestan por otro concepto: los espacios abiertos sin paredes, con la cocina abierta al resto de la casa y un espacio versátil para las comidas que, en función de las necesidades, puede convertirse en una mesa de trabajo para niños y mayores. Todos los diseños de cocina actuales abogan por espacios cómodos y luminosos en los que preparar la comida y sentarse a la mesa se convierte en un auténtico placer.

HISTORY
THE

OF
KITCHEN

L'histoire
de la cuisine
Geschichte
der Küche

Historia de
la cocina

Human history evolves alongside eating habits. Two million years ago, Australopitecus was solely concerned with gathering food. Its successor, Peking Man, incorporated meat into a previously vegetarian diet, altering what would later be the eating habits of human beings. With the revolution of the hunt and the ingestion of meat appeared the first rudimentary techniques for roasting. The bonfire was a consequence of the use of the first stone implements. The discovery that fire could be controlled solved the problem of cold, and fire thus became indispensable to the creation of the earliest cooked dishes. Neanderthal man extended the range of its recipes by using heated stones, a first step towards the invention of frying.

The invention of the kitchen was an important discovery, bringing pre-historic man a step closer to civilization. We can

Die historische Entwicklung des Menschen verläuft parallel zur Entwicklung seiner Essgewohnheiten. Der Australopithecus befasste sich vor zwei Millionen Jahren ausschließlich mit dem Sammeln von Nahrung. Sein Nachfolger, der Pekingmensch, brachte Fleisch auf den bis dahin vegetarischen Speisezettel und löste so eine allmähliche Veränderung der menschlichen Essgepflogenheiten aus. Die Weiterentwicklung der Jagd und der Fleischverzehr führten zu ersten Ansätzen, Lebensmittel zu garen. Die Entstehung der Holzfeuerstelle resultierte aus dem Gebrauch der ersten Steinwerkzeuge. Die Entdeckung, dass Feuer zu kontrollieren war, löste das Problem der Kälte und machte es zu einem unentbehrlichen Hilfsmittel zur Zubereitung der ersten Gerichte. Der Neanderthaler erweiterte die Auswahl seiner Kochrezepte durch die Verwendung heißer

L'histoire humaine a évolué parallèlement aux habitudes alimentaires. Il y a deux millions d'années, l'australopithèque avait comme unique occupation la récolte de la nourriture. Son successeur, l'homme de Pékin ajouta à sa diète végétarienne la consommation de viande, changeant ainsi progressivement les habitudes alimentaires de l'être humain. Avec la révolution amenée par la chasse et la consommation de viande, apparurent les premières techniques rudimentaires pour la rôtir. Le bûcher fût le résultat de l'utilisation des premiers outils de pierre. La découverte de pouvoir contrôler le feu permit de résoudre le problème du froid et il devint ainsi indispensable à la création des premiers plats cuisinés. L'homme du Neandertal étendit la variété de ses recettes en utilisant des pierres chauffées, ce qui précéda à l'invention de la friture.

La historia humana evoluciona paralelamente con los hábitos alimentarios. Hace dos millones de años, el Australopitecus se dedicaba solamente a recolectar alimentos. Su sucesor, el Hombre de Pekín, incorporó a la dieta vegetariana el consumo de carne, cambiando progresivamente los hábitos alimenticios del ser humano. Con la revolución de la caza y la ingestión de carne aparecieron las primeras técnicas rudimentarias para asar los alimentos. La hoguera de leña fue consecuencia de la utilización de los primeros utensilios de piedra. El descubrimiento de la posibilidad de controlar el fuego solucionó el problema del frío y se convirtió en instrumento imprescindible para los primeros guisos. Más tarde, el hombre de Neanderthal amplió la variedad de sus recetas con la utilización de piedras calientes, paso previo a la invención de la fritura.

state that the home and civilization were conceived around the kitchen. While in the Neolithic Age the kitchen consisted of only a hole in the ground, already this area was considered the center of the home. Fire defined the first stage in the evolution of the kitchen, since it was the only resource available to cook meals and heat the home. With fire, cereals could be toasted and meat and fish could be roasted and smoked. Fire also permitted discovery of new flavors, while at the same time prolonging conservation. Practical cooking implements were invented to manipulate foods. The first

Steine, was als erster Schritt auf dem Weg hin zur Erfindung des Bratens gilt.

Die Erfindung der Küche war eine äußerst bedeutende Entdeckung und hob die menschliche Existenz auf ein zivilisierteres Niveau. Man könnte behaupten, dass das Haus und die Zivilisation als solche um die Küche herum entstanden. Bereits in der Jungsteinzeit bildete sie den Mittelpunkt des Heims, obwohl sie im Grunde nur aus einem Erdloch bestand, in dem das Feuer geschürt wurde. Mit dem Feuer beginnt die Geschichte der Küche, denn nur mit Feuer war das Garen von Lebensmitteln und das

L'invention de la cuisinière fût une découverte importante rapprochant ainsi l'homme préhistorique de l'être humain actuel. Nous pouvons affirmer que le foyer et la civilisation même naquirent autour d'elle. Pendant la période néolithique, elle consistait simplement en un tout dans le sol dans lequel ont faisait un feu et qui était considéré comme le centre du foyer. Le feu fût la première étape dans l'évolution de la cuisine du fait que c'était l'unique ressource disponible pour cuire les repas et chauffer la maison. Grâce au feu on pouvait dorer les céréales, rôtir et fumer la viande et le poisson, ce qui permit prolonger leur conservation et de découvrir d'autres saveurs. Des ustensiles de cuisine

La invención de la cocina supuso un descubrimiento de gran importancia y elevó la existencia del hombre. Podríamos afirmar que la casa y la civilización misma nacieron en torno a la cocina. En el neolítico, aunque se reducía a un agujero en el suelo donde se encendía el fuego, ya suponía el centro del hogar. El fuego constituye una primera etapa para la cocina, puesto que constituía el único recurso para cocinar los alimentos y calentar la casa. El fuego podía tostar los cereales, asar y ahumar la carne y el pescado, permitía conocer otros sabores y, a la vez, prolongaba su conservación. Para poder manipular los alimentos inventaron elementos que resultaban prácticos para la cocción. Los primeros

were a kind of leather vessel into which water was added and pre-heated stones introduced. Later, earthen bowls capable of being placed on the fire appeared, in addition to implements such as cane rods used for roasting fish. In Turkey, archaeologists discovered a Neolithic kitchen with water receptacles, plates and even an implement for heating food resembling a fondue. Aztec civilization utilized a multitude of domestic tools. It was the Aztecs who introduced the concept of the kitchen-dining room, situated in the center of the home where the fire remained permanently lit. The ancient Egyptians possessed fertile fields with abundant agriculture. As such, they were able to dedicate their time to activities

Heizen des Hauses möglich. Es diente zum Rösten von Getreide und zum Braten und Räuchern von Fleisch und Fisch; erschloss neue Geschmacksrichtungen und verlängerte die Haltbarkeit der Nahrung. Zur Verarbeitung der Lebensmittel wurden praktische Geräte erfunden. Zu den ersten gehörte eine Art Lederbehältnis, in das Wasser gefüllt und zuvor im Feuer erhitzte Steine gelegt wurden. Später kamen Schüsseln aus Ton auf, die auf das Feuer gestellt werden konnten, sowie andere Geräte wie dünne Gerten, auf denen Fisch gebraten wurde. Archäologen entdeckten in der Türkei eine jungsteinzeitliche Küche mit Wassergefäßen, Schüsseln und sogar einen Kocher, der an einen heutigen Fonduetopf erinnert. Die Aztekenkulturen benutzten bereits eine Vielzahl von Hausgeräten und führten das Konzept der in der Mitte des Hauses liegenden Wohnküche mit

pratiques furent inventés pour manipuler les aliments. Les premiers étaient des sortes de récipients en cuire auxquels on ajoutait de l'eau et dans lesquels on introduisait des pierres préalablement chauffées au feu. Plus tard, des bols de terre pouvant être placés sur le feu firent leur apparition de même que d'autres instruments tels que des baguettes en rotin pour rôtir le poisson. Des archéologues ont découvert en Turquie, une cuisine néolithique avec des récipients pour l'eau, des fontaines de même que des réchauds pour la nourriture ressemblant aux réchauds à fondue. Les Aztèques utilisaient déjà une multitude d'ustensiles ménagers et ce sont eux qui introduirent l'idée de cuisine/salle à manger située au centre de la maison et où un feu brûlait en permanence. Les Egyptiens disposaient de terres très fertiles et d'une agriculture abondante, de ce fait

instrumentos fueron una especie de vasijas de cuero a las que se añadía agua y en donde se introducían piedras previamente calentadas por el fuego. Más tarde aparecerían los cuencos de tierra que podían colocarse sobre el fuego, además de otros instrumentos, como las varillas de caña para asar el pescado. Los arqueólogos han encontrado en Turquía una cocina neolítica con recipientes para el agua, fuentes e incluso un calentador de comidas parecido a una fondue. Las civilizaciones aztecas ya utilizan multitud de enseres domésticos e introducen el concepto de cocina-comedor que se sitúa en el centro de la casa, donde el fuego permanecía siempre encendido. Los egipcios disponían de tierras muy fértiles con abundante agricultura, por lo que podían dedicar su tiempo a otras actividades no relacionadas con la subsistencia; así crearon, en-

unrelated to subsistence, inventing, among others, new wood and stone implements and tools in the process.

The Greek and Roman cultures brought us three new cooking techniques: roasting, boiling and stewing. They also introduced new materials into the kitchen such as glass bottles, wooden pitchers and decorated ceramics. With only a built-in burner and a hole to allow for the extraction of fumes, the Romans devoted very little space to this room. The burner was situated on top of a kind of brick bench and there was an opening where the firewood could be stowed away. It was in a fixed place normally behind the atrium. In this period the cooking procedure consisted of using a round

ständig brennendem Feuer ein. Die Ägypter verfügten über äußerst fruchtbare Böden mit einer stark entwickelten Landwirtschaft und konnten ihre Zeit somit auch anderen, nicht dem reinen Überleben dienenden Tätigkeiten widmen, wobei sie unter anderem neue Instrumente und Gerätschaften aus Holz und Stein erfanden.

Griechen und Römer führten drei Grundtechniken der Kochkunst ein: Braten, Kochen und Schmoren. Daneben entwickelten sie neue Küchengegenstände wie die Glasflasche, den Holzkrug und verzierte Keramik. Die Römer gestanden der Küche nur wenig Platz zu: eine gemauerte Feuerstelle und eine Öffnung als Rauchabzug. Die Feuerstelle

ils purent consacrer une partie de leurs activités, non seulement à subsister mais également tas inventer de nouveaux instruments et outils de bois et de pierre.

Les cultures grecques et romaines connaissaient trois techniques de cuisson : rôtir, bouillir et mijoter. Ils introduirent d'autres matériaux dans la cuisine tels que les bouteilles de verre, des cruches de bois et la céramique décorée. Les romains ne consacraient que très peu de place à cette pièce ayant un fourneau et un trou permettant à la fumée de s'échapper. Il était constitué d'un banc de briques sur lequel ont faisait le feu et un creux où l'on pouvait ranger le bois. Il se trouvait à un endroit

tre otros, nuevos instrumentos y enseres de madera y piedra.

Con las culturas griega y romana se conocieron tres técnicas base de cocción: el asado, el hervido y el guisado, además de añadir nuevos materiales a la cocina, como la botella de vidrio, las jarras de madera y la cerámica decorada. Los romanos dedicaban muy poco espacio a esta estancia, con un fogón de obra y un agujero para la salida de humos. Constaba de un banco de ladrillo sobre el que se hacía el fuego y un hueco donde podía almacenarse la leña. Se situaba donde quedaba un espacio fijo, normalmente detrás del atrio. La técnica utilizada para cocinar en esta época era hervir los alimentos en una

terracotta pot in which the food was boiled.

Beginning in the Lower Middle Ages, utensils made of other materials such as brass, copper or iron were utilized. These were placed directly on the coals although supports such as trivets were also used, so that there was not direct contact.

During the Middle Ages food was cooked over the fire of the chimney which was usually very high and broad. The thirteenth century marked the appearance of kitchens with ovens and tables. Only the wealthiest of families availed themselves of ovens and burners. The utensils used were long-handled pots and frying pans, and huge cooking pots with brass handles.

While in the most rural areas people and animals shared space under the same roof (so that the heat of the

bestand aus aufgeschichteten Ziegelsteinen, auf denen das Feuer entzündet wurde, und einem Hohlraum, in dem man Holz aufbewahrte. Sie lag an einem befestigten Ort, meistens hinter dem Atrium. Die in dieser Epoche übliche Kochtechnik bestand darin, die Lebensmittel in meist runden Terrakottatöpfen zu kochen.

Im frühen Mittelalter nahm der Gebrauch von Küchengeräten aus anderen Materialien wie Messing, Kupfer oder Eisen zu, die direkt auf die Glut gestellt wurden, oder an Halterungen wie dem Dreifuß befestigt wurden, um den direkten Kontakt mit dem Feuer zu vermeiden.

Im Mittelalter wurde über dem Feuer des Kamins gekocht, der meist sehr hoch und breit war. Ab dem 13. Jahrhundert stattete man die Küchen mit kleinen Kochherden und Tischen aus.

fixe, généralement derrière l'atrium. La technique de cuisine utilisée à cette époque consistait à faire bouillir la nourriture dans des grandes marmites rondes en terre cuite.

A partir du moyen âge ont utilisa des ustensiles en laiton, en cuivre ou en fer. On les plaçait directement sur les braises ou parfois, pour éviter un contact direct, sur un support.

Au moyen âge les aliments se cuisaient sur le feu de cheminée qui étaient généralement très hautes et larges. Au 13ième siècle, des cuisines ayant des cuisinières et des tables firent leur apparition. Seules les familles aisées pouvaient s'offrir de telles cuisinières. On employait de grandes casseroles et poêles à manches longs et de grandes marmites de laiton avec des poignées.

Dans les régions rurales les gens et les animaux étaient sous le même toit (la

olla de terracota, que solía tener forma redondeada.

A partir de la baja edad media aumenta la utilización de enseres realizados con otros materiales como el latón, el cobre o el hierro, que se colocaban directamente sobre brasas, aunque también se usaban soportes como trébedes para que el contacto no fuera directo.

En la edad media, los alimentos se cocinaban sobre el fuego de la chimenea, que acostumbraba a ser muy alta y amplia. En el siglo XIII se empiezan a instalar cocinas con hornillos y mesas. Sólo las familias más adineradas disponen de horno y fogones. Los elementos utilizados para la cocina son cazos y sartenes con mango muy largo y grandes marmitas de latón con asas.

Mientras en las regiones más campesinas las personas y los animales conviven bajo el mismo techo (con la intención de

animals would warm up the house), beginning in the sixteenth and seventeenth centuries, a profound renovation in rural architecture began to occur. We see the appearance of a place under roof for storing grain, and a common room with a fire. In the wealthiest residences there is even a space for the oven and even a chamber for making bread. Little by little the place reserved for the fire becomes farther from the center of the room to become situated

Nur wohlhabendere Familien konnten sich Backöfen und Herde leisten. Die vorherrschenden Küchengerätschaften waren Töpfe und Bratpfannen mit sehr langen Stielen sowie große Messingtöpfe mit Henkeln.

Während die Menschen in den ländlicheren Gebieten weiterhin mit den Tieren unter einem Dach lebten (um die tierische Wärme für das Haus zu nutzen), kam es ab dem 16. und 17. Jahrhundert zu einer grundlegenden Erneuerung der

chaleur du bétail chauffait la maison). A partir du 16ième – 17ième siècle il y eut de grands changements dans l'architecture rurale. On voit l'apparition d'une salle destinée à entreposer le grain et d'une pièce commune avec un feu. Dans les maisons plus aisées il y a une place réservée à la cuisinière ainsi qu'une pièce pour faire le pain. Peu à peu l'endroit réservé au feu s'éloigne du centre de la pièce pour être placé contre une parois ce qui amena la création de cheminées

aprovechar el calor del ganado para la casa), a partir de los siglos XVI–VII empieza a producirse una profunda renovación de la arquitectura rural, con espacio para guardar el grano bajo el techo y una sala común con fuego, e incluso, en las casas más ricas, un espacio para el horno con una cámara para amasar el pan. Poco a poco, la zona donde se ubica el fuego se aleja del centro de la habitación a una pared, creando chimeneas (aparecen en el siglo XVIII). Esta acción

on a wall, which is the creation of the chimney (it appears in the eighteenth century). This marks a change in the distribution of the house. The kitchen starts to take shape as its own space, to later become an independent room. It is separated and almost hidden from the rest of the house, although ventilated and well distributed. It also contains a high, broad chimney, burners on which hot coals are placed for frying, and work tables where the food can be prepared. In

ländlichen Architektur. Es kamen Räume für die Lagerung des Getreides unter dem Dach und Gemeinschaftsräume mit Feuerstelle auf, in den reicheren Häusern sogar Plätze für den Backofen mit einem Fach zum Brotbacken. Nach und nach verlegte man die Feuerstelle aus der Mitte des Raums hin zur Wand. Der Hauskamin entstand im 18. Jahrhundert. Diese Veränderung löste eine Verschiebung in der Aufteilung des Hauses aus: Die Küche erhielt allmählich ihren

(elles apparaissent au 18ième siècle). Cela marqua un changement dans la répartition des pièces et la cuisine commence à prendre forme comme espace propre, devenant plus tard une pièce indépendante. Elle est séparée et presque cachée au sein de la maison. Elle jouit d'une aération et est bien agencée avec des cheminées hautes et larges, avec des fourneaux à bois et des tables de travail permettant de préparer la nourriture. Dans les maisons bourgeoises il y a

inicia un cambio en la distribución de la casa, y la cocina empieza a tomar forma como espacio propio y, más tarde, como estancia independiente. Se reserva como habitación alejada y casi escondida, aunque ventilada y bien distribuida, con chimeneas altas y amplias, con fogones sobre los que se depositan brasas para freír y mesas de trabajo para los alimentos. En las casas burguesas se incluye un patio para limpiar la carne y el pescado y una zona más fresca reservada

bourgeois houses a patio for cleaning meat and fish is included, and a cooler area where food can be stored. A large kitchen with light, an oven, burners, a well and a sink are considered necessary.

In middle-class families it is the women who do the cooking while they delegate other household activities to the maids. In well-to-do homes cooks and servants abound. It is interesting to point out that in the modern age in the kitchens of the wealthiest families, men were preferred since they were considered to be cleaner, more loyal and more competent, according to a text by Francesco Tanara in the seventeenth century. In the noblest of residences, not only were the kitchen personnel male, they were of a relatively high social class, the reason being that the master feared poisoning and so he required servants who could afford him total trust.

eigenen Platz, später sogar ihren eigenen Raum. Sie war abgelegen, aber belüftet und gut aufgeteilt, mit hohen und breiten Kaminen. Es gab Feuerstellen mit Glut zum Braten und Arbeitstische für die Lebensmittel. Bürgerliche Häuser waren mit einem Innenhof, in dem Fleisch und Fisch gereinigt wurden, sowie einem kühlen Bereich zur Aufbewahrung von Lebensmitteln ausgestattet. Eine große Küche mit Licht, Ofen und Herd, Brunnenanlage und Spülstein wurde als notwendig erachtet.

In Familien der Mittelklasse war die Hausfrau für die Essenszubereitung, die Dienstmädchen für die übrigen Hausarbeiten zuständig. In den Häusern der Adligen gab es Scharen von Köchen und Bediensteten. Als Kuriosum ist anzumerken, dass die Küchen der bedeutenden Familien in der Neuzeit abgeschirmte Bereiche waren, in denen man Männern

même un patio pour nettoyer la viande et le poisson ainsi qu'un endroit plus frais pour emmagasiner la nourriture. Une grande cuisine éclairée avec des fourneaux, un puits et un évier sont considérés comme indispensable.

Dans les familles de classe moyenne, ce sont les femmes qui font la cuisine, déléguant au personnel les autres activités domestiques. Dans les maisons plus aisées, les cuisiniers et les employés de maison abondent. Il est curieux de signaler que, selon un écrit de Francesco Tanara du 17ième siècle, dans les temps modernes, les cuisines dans les grandes familles étaient réservées aux hommes qu'on considérait comme plus propres, fiables et compétents. Dans les demeures nobles le personnel s'occupant de la cuisine était unique-

para almacenar los alimentos. Se considera necesaria una cocina grande con luz, horno y fogón, pozo y fregadero.

En las familias de clase media, las mujeres son las que guisan mientras delegan en las criadas las demás actividades domésticas. En las casas nobles abundan los cocineros y sirvientes. Es curioso señalar que en la edad moderna las cocinas de las grandes familias eran espacios reservados donde se prefería a los hombres, puesto que se les consideraba más limpios, fieles y competentes, según se desprende de un escrito de Francesco Tanara en el siglo XVII. En las viviendas más nobles, el personal que se ocupaba de la cocina, además de ser masculino, era de elevada condición social, puesto que el amo temía los envenamientos y necesitaba un servicio totalmente fiel.

Not in all homes and in all countries was a professional cuisine required. Although cooking was appreciated, it was an activity, which was still considered menial. The kitchen was a secondary room reserved for the servants. In homes without a cook, one of the maids would also take charge of the cooking. In middle and lower class homes, women generally took charge of all of the household chores, including the cooking, which they realized with rudimentary means. In some homes the kitchen was limited to simply a stewpot hanging from a chain over a hearth on the floor. From the eighteenth century on, a traditional trivet or brick burners were used, which raised the stewpot over the hot coal. Little by little around 1750 the first economical metal stoves appeared. When married woman took over the household chores from the

den Vorzug gab. Ihnen sagte man nach, sauberer, treuer und kompetenter zu sein, wie aus einer Schrift aus dem 17. Jahrhundert von Francesco Tanara hervorgeht. In den großen Adelshäusern war das Küchenpersonal nicht nur männlich, sondern auch gesellschaftlich besser gestellt, da der Hausherr Vergiftungen fürchtete und aus diesem Grunde absolut treues Dienstpersonal benötigte.

Nicht in allen Ländern und Häusern achtete man auf einen professionellen Service. Oftmals war das Kochen, auch wenn man kulinarische Genüsse zu schätzen wusste, von zweitrangiger Bedeutung. Die Küche galt als untergeordneter Raum und war den Bediensteten vorbehalten. In manchen Häusern, in denen es keinen Koch gab, musste ein normalerweise andere Hausarbeiten verrichtendes Dienstmädchen auch für die gesamte Familie kochen. Im Allgemeinen

ment masculine et de bonne condition sociale, les maîtres craignant d'être empoisonnés et désirant un service de toute confiance.

Ni tous les pays ni toutes les maisons requièrent un service professionnel, bien qu'appréciant les activités culinaires, le fait de cuisiner était purement servile. La cuisine était un endroit de deuxième rang réservée au personnel. Dans les maisons n'ayant pas de cuisinier, l'un des membres du personnel chargé des tâches domestiques devait également faire la cuisine pour toute la famille.

Ni todos los países ni todas las viviendas requerían de un servicio profesional. En muchos de ellos, a pesar de que se apreciara la actividad culinaria, la acción de cocinar era puramente servil. La cocina era entendida como un espacio de condición secundaria, reservado a los criados. En las casas donde no había cocinero, alguna criada encargada de las tareas domésticas de la casa debía también cocinar para toda la familia. Y en general, las mujeres de clase social media y baja seguían encargándose de todas las tareas domésticas con medios

servants, the kitchen evolved, though very slowly. Elements, which made it more comfortable, started to become incorporated: kitchen furniture, copper or marble sinks and even hot water tanks. Women started to take decisions regarding the equipment of the kitchen whereas the servants simply received orders.

Kitchen materials experienced constant evolution throughout the nineteenth century. At the start of the century kitchen stoves were made of bricks and wood was used for burning. The burner did not have a chimney and fumes would fill the room. A bit later on iron stoves with the burner incorporated, appeared. Around 1850 the first gas stoves made their appearance and gradually started replacing the ones using coal. The arrival of gas meant the beginning of the mechanization of the house. These stoves did not immediately

waren die Frauen der mittleren und unteren Gesellschaftsschicht weiterhin für sämtliche Hausarbeiten zuständig, für die sie nur über einfachste Hilfsmittel verfügten. In einigen Häusern bestand die Küche nur aus einem Kochtopf, der an einer Kette über der Feuerstelle hing; gekocht wurde auf ebener Erde. Dies änderte sich ab dem 18. Jahrhundert mit der Verwendung des traditionellen Dreifußes (über einem Kohlenfeuer) oder den Ziegelherden. Erst nach und nach wurden um das Jahr 1750 die wirtschaftlichen Metallherde eingeführt. Als die Hausfrau die häuslichen Tätigkeiten des Dienstpersonals übernahm, setzten sich langsam einige Neuerungen durch, die den Komfort erhöhten: Küchenmöbel, Spülbecken aus Kupfer oder Marmor, sogar Heißwassertanks. Die Frau des Hauses konnte auf die Ausstattung der Küche aktiv Einfluss nehmen,

Généralement les femmes de classe sociale moyenne et basse s'occupent de toutes les tâches ménagères avec des moyens très rudimentaires. Dans certaines maisons la cuisine se résume à une marmite pendue à une chaîne au-dessus du foyer, placé à même le sol. A partir du 18ième siècle cela changera avec l'utilisation de trépieds et de constructions en briques chauffées à la braise. Peu à peu vers 1750, les premières cuisinières en métal font leur apparition. Quand la femme mariée remplaça les servants dans les tâches domestiques, on nota une évolution de la cuisine. Lentement on y intégra des éléments la rendant plus commode : meubles de cuisine, lavoirs en cuivre ou en pierre, de même que des réservoirs d'eau chaude. La femme prend des décisions d'ordre ménagère alors que jusqu'à maintenant les serviteurs ne faisaient que recevoir des ordres.

Au 19ième siècle, le matériel de cuisine est en évolution constante. Au début

muy rudimentarios. En algunas casas, la cocina se limitaba a un puchero colgado de una cadena sobre el hogar, una actividad a ras de suelo que a partir del siglo XVIII se elevaba utilizando los tradicionales trébedes (que se calentaban con brasas de carbón), o fogones de ladrillo. Y poco a poco, aproximadamente hacia el año 1750, fueron apareciendo las cocinas económicas de metal. Cuando la mujer casada relevó a los sirvientes en las tareas domésticas, esta habitación fue evolucionando por necesidad, aunque muy lentamente, integrando elementos que podían hacerla más cómoda: muebles de cocina, lavaderos de cobre o mármol e incluso depósitos con agua caliente. La mujer podía ahora interferir en las decisiones referentes al equipamiento de la cocina, mientras que los sirvientes sólo recibían órdenes.

während dies den Bediensteten als reinen Befehlsempfängern nicht möglich war.

Im 19. Jahrhundert war die Küche Gegenstand stetiger Entwicklung. Anfänglich bestand ein Herd aus Ziegeln und für das Feuer verwendete man Holzkohle, wobei noch kein Rauchabzug vorhanden war, sodass sich der Rauch im ganzen Raum verteilte. Bald sollte es den geschlossenen Eisenherd geben. Mit der Einführung der ersten Gasherde um 1850 begann die Mechanisierung des Haushaltes. Trotz der Vorteile dieser Herdart ersetzten sie nur allmählich die Kohleherde. Es wurde mindestens weitere 50 Jahre lang mit Kohle oder Holz gekocht, bis sie vorherrschend wurden. Die ersten Gasherde wiesen noch ein dem Kohleherd ähnliches Design, es gab sogar Modelle, die beide Systeme miteinander kombinierten.

Sich in den Küchen im Laufe der Jahre abwechselnde Dekorationsstile wurden zur Inspiration für die aktuellen Modelle.

become popular and for at least 50 more years cooking was done with coal or wood. When gas stoves started to become predominant, the design was similar to the coal ones and some models allowed the two systems to be combined.

Over the years we have seen the succession of different decorating styles,

du siècle, la cuisinière était en briques et la combustion réalisée au charbon de bois. Les fourneaux n'ayant pas de cheminée, la fumée se dispersait dans la pièce. Rapidement des cuisinières en métal avec four intérieur firent leur apparition. A partir de 1850, on voit les premières cuisinières à gaz, qui remplacent lentement celles au charbon. L'arrivée du gaz marqua le début de la mécanisation de la maison. Les avantages de ce nouveau type de cuisinière ne fût pas populaire dès le début. Et l'on continua à faire la cuisine au bois et au charbon pendant une cinquantaine d'années encore. Quand les cuisinières à gaz

Durante el siglo XIX el material de cocina es objeto de constante evolución. En sus inicios, la cocina se construye con ladrillos y la combustión se realiza con carbón de leña, aunque el fogón no dispone de chimenea y los humos se esparcen por toda la habitación. Pronto aparecerá la cocina de hierro con fogón interior. A partir de 1850 aparecen las primeras cocinas de gas, que lentamente van sustituyendo las antiguas cocinas de carbón. La llegada del gas significó el inicio de la mecanización de la casa. Las ventajas de este tipo de cocinas no se hicieron populares de inmediato, por lo que durante por lo menos otros

expressed through kitchens, and these styles have become the source of inspiration for present-day models of kitchens. It is not easy to imitate or recuperate a style of decoration, as it is essential that the style adapt well to the present-day environment and requirements. A good option is to recreate a style by combining old and contemporary elements. To do this it is important to know what elements characterize a particular style. In kitchens the dominant

Das Imitieren oder die Wiederbelebung eines Stils ist nicht leicht, denn er muss sich auch an die jeweilige Umgebung und die aktuellen Bedürfnisse anpassen. Ein guter Ansatz ist die Kombination von alten und modernen Elementen. Unerlässlich ist zu wissen, was den jeweiligen Stil charakterisiert. Zur Zeit sind sowohl auf dem Land als auch in Stadtwohnungen, in denen natürliche Räume nachempfunden werden, Küchen im Landhaus-Stil vorherrschend, die durch

commencèrent à s'établir, leur apparence était la même que celle des cuisinières à charbon. Certains modèles combinaient les deux systèmes.

Les différents styles de décoration se sont succédés au fil des années dans la cuisine, pour devenir la source d'inspiration des modèles actuels. Imiter ou essayer de retrouver un style de décoration n'est pas une tâche facile du fait qu'il est important de l'adapter aux alentours et aux besoins actuels. Une bonne solution

cincuenta años se siguió cocinando con carbón o leña. Cuando las cocinas de gas empezaron a implantarse tenían un diseño muy similar a las de carbón, incluso algunos modelos combinaban ambos sistemas.

Los diferentes estilos decorativos se han ido sucediendo en las cocinas, hasta ser el punto de inspiración de los modelos actuales. Imitar o intentar recuperar un estilo decorativo no es tarea fácil, puesto que debe adaptarse al entorno y

tendency (especially in rural homes or in urban residences which recreate natural surroundings) is the rustic style. The love for rural traditions influences kitchens of this type. This is the purest of all styles since it has its origins in the village lifestyle and is an adaptation from popular customs. To imitate a rustic style, you need to choose simple pieces made from simple though robust and solid materials, since this is what peasants used in their country houses beginning in the seventeenth century. In the most modest of homes, the furniture was made from the same materials available to them in their work. The pure English rustic style made its appearance in the eighteenth century whereas in the same period in North America, the colonial American style emerged. A strong, local handcraft influence and light, clean spaces characterized it.

ländliche Traditionen beeinflusst sind. Diese reinste aller Stilrichtungen geht auf die dörfliche Lebensweise zurück und passt sich gleichzeitig den populären Gepflogenheiten an. Um diesen rustikalen Stil zu imitieren, verwendet man schlichte Stücke aus einfachen, robusten Materialien, wie sie ab dem 17. Jahrhundert in den Bauernhäusern üblich waren. In den bescheidensten Häusern bestanden seinerzeit die Möbel aus dem Material, das auch bei der Arbeit verwendet wurde. Im 18. Jahrhundert bildete sich der rein rustikale englische Stil und in Nordamerika der amerikanische Kolonialstil heraus, der stark lokale handwerkliche Einflüsse sowie schlichte und sauber wirkende Räume aufweist.

Der rustikale Stil basiert auf dem Einsatz von natürlichen Materialien wie Holz, Schmiedeeisen, Ton und Stein. In ländlichen Häusern verwendet man für

pour recréer un style est de combiner quelques éléments antiques et contemporains. De ce fait il est important de connaître les caractéristiques propres à chaque style. Dans la cuisine, la tendance prédominante (spécialement pour les maisons de campagne et les habitations urbaines désirant recréer un espace naturel) est le style rustique. Le goût de la tradition paysanne influence une cuisine de ce type. Il s'agit du style le plus pur de tous du fait qu'il a son origine dans la façon de vivre dans les villages, et s'adapte aux coutumes populaires. Pour imiter le style rustique on choisit des pièces simples et des matériaux solides et robustes étant ceux utilisés à partir du 17ième siècle par les paysans pour leurs maisons de campagne. Dans les maisons plus modestes, les meubles sont réalisés avec les matériaux dont on dispose pour travailler. Le style purement

a las necesidades actuales. Una buena opción para recrear un estilo consiste en conciliar algunos elementos antiguos con piezas actuales. Y para ello, es importante conocer qué elementos caracterizan cada uno de los estilos. En la cocina, la tendencia imperante (especialmente en casas rurales o en viviendas urbanas que recrean espacios naturales) es el estilo rústico. El gusto por la tradición rural influye en una cocina de este tipo. Se trata del estilo más puro de todos los que existen, puesto que tiene su origen en la forma de vivir del pueblo y se adapta a las costumbres populares. Para imitar el estilo rústico deben elegirse piezas simples, con materiales sencillos aunque robustos y sólidos, puesto que son los que han ido utilizando desde siglo XVII los campesinos de las casas de campo. En las casas más modestas, los muebles se realizaban con

The rustic style is based on the use of natural materials such as wood, wrought iron, earthenware and stone. It uses shapes appropriate to country life and wood such as oak, which is less refined than the walnut or mahogany, commonly employed in decoration styles in the city. In some countries there is a tendency to make it more elaborate and in other countries they use design furniture which has a more robust and coarser appearance. At any rate, the intention is to

das Landleben geeignete Formen und Hölzer wie Eiche, anstelle des eleganteren Nussbaum oder Mahagoni, die beide für Stilrichtungen aus dem städtischen Bereich charakteristisch sind. In einigen Ländern hat der rustikale Stil eine gewisse Tendenz zum Überladenenen, in anderen bevorzugt man Möbel mit groberen Formen und robustem Äußeren. Ziel ist immer, die Lebensweise auf dem Land nachzuempfinden, wo die Landwirtschaft die vorherrschende Wirtschaftsweise war. Das hier robustere und solidere Mobiliar musste sich an die harten, bescheidenen Lebensumstände der Bauern anpassen. Es kommt daher mit einfachen, den funktionalen häuslichen Anforderungen entsprechenden Formen

rustique anglais apparaît au 18ième siè-cle de même que le style colonial d'A-mérique du Nord qui se caractérise par une forte influence de l'artisanat local et des espaces légers et nets.

Le style rustique est basé sur l'utilisa-tion de matériaux naturels comme le bois, le fer forgé, la terre cuite et la pier-re. Les maisons rustiques utilisent des formes propres à la vie de campagne avec des bois tels que le chêne, moins raffiné que le noyer ou l'acajou employé

los mismos materiales de los que dispo-nían para trabajar. El estilo puramente rústico inglés aparece en el siglo XVIII, mientras en la misma época en Nortea-mérica surge el estilo colonial america-no, que destaca por una fuerte influen-cia de la artesanía local y espacios ligeros y limpios.

El estilo rústico se basa en la utiliza-ción de materiales naturales como la madera, el hierro forjado, el barro y la piedra. Las casas rústicas utilizaban

recreate a style that defines a way of life in the rural areas where agriculture was the mainstay of economic activity. The furniture was more robust and solid since it had to adapt to the harshness of the life and to the modesty of the peasants. The shapes were simple and sober and had a practical, functional and domestic appearance, which were distinct from more classical aesthetic designs.

In rustic kitchens you can find cutting boards for cold cuts, benches and very simple and functional sideboards and glass cabinets. The items and furniture, sometimes inherited or obtained in flea markets or antique shops, is painted, waxed and restored to look like new. Wooden rafters, earthenware floor tiles, and simple and very functional furniture characterize rustic style. This is combined with decorative items reminiscent

aus und entfernt sich von den klassischeren Ausdrucksformen.

In rustikalen Küchen finden sich äußerst praktische Arbeitstische, Sitzbänke, Anrichten und Vitrinen. Möbel dieser Art kann man auf Versteigerungen oder Flohmärkten erstehen oder man kann ein Erbstück restaurieren, firnissen, wachsen oder abbeizen und umfunktionieren. Charakteristisch sind außerdem Holzbalkendecken, Böden aus Stein oder Terrakottafliesen, schlichte und funktionelle Möbel sowie an Küchen auf dem Land erinnernde Dekorationsgegenstände: Töpfe, alte Teekannen oder Krüge, Obst, Wiesenblumen in Körben oder zum Trocknen aufgehängte Kräuterbündel und im Kamin die dazugehörigen eisernen Gerätschaften.

Küchen im klassischen Stil sind ausgewogene Entwürfe, die sich durch eine Kombination von Eleganz, Komfort und

pour d'autres styles et plus fréquemment en ville. Dans certains pays on a tendance à plus le charger utilisant un design plus grossier et d'aspect plus robuste. L'intention étant de recréer un style définissant le mode de vie à la campagne où l'agriculture était la principale activité économique. Le mobilier est plus solide et robuste devant s'adapter à la dureté des conditions et à l'humilité paysanne. Il a les formes simples et sobres que requière un aspect pratique et fonctionnel se distinguant des designs esthétique plus classique.

Les cuisines rustiques ont des établis, des tables des bancs, des buffets et des vitrines très simples et fonctionnelles. On peut en hériter ou les trouver sur les marchés aux puces ou dans des magasins d'antiquités. Ils sont remis à neuf biens restaurés vernis et cirés. Le style rustique se définit par des plafonds en

formas apropiadas para la vida del campo, con maderas como el roble –menos refinada que el nogal o la caoba, que se empleaban en otros estilos más utilizados en las ciudades–. Algunos países tienden a recargarlo más y en otros se utilizan muebles de diseño más toscos y de aspecto robusto. En cualquier caso, se trata de recrear un estilo que define la forma de vida de las zonas rurales, donde la agricultura fue la principal actividad económica. El mobiliario era más robusto y sólido, puesto que debía adaptarse a la dureza de las condiciones y a la humildad de los campesinos, y se presenta con formas sencillas y sobrias que requieren un aspecto práctico, funcional y doméstico, alejándose de los diseños estéticos más clásicos.

Las cocinas rústicas emplean mesas tocineras, bancos, aparadores y vitrinas muy simples y funcionales, que pueden

of old country kitchens: pots, teapots, old jugs, fruit, wild flowers in baskets or bunches of herbs hanging out to dry, and iron utensils hanging on the chimney ready for use.

A classical kitchen is another decorative option. This is an eclectic style, which stands out thanks to its elegance, comfort and the high quality of the furniture. With refined lines and a purely bourgeois decoration, it recreates the atmosphere of a period. Sometimes a

hochwertigem Mobiliar auszeichnen. Sie stehen für die Wiederbelebung eines zeittypischen Ambientes mit raffinierten Formen und eindeutig bürgerlichen Elementen. So kann man z. B. eine klassische Atmosphäre schaffen, indem man einige für die Zeit typische Stücke auswählt, für dezente Beleuchtung sorgt oder schlichtes Mobiliar auf elegante Weise arrangiert. In der Küche genügt es nicht, dass das Mobiliar eine Stilepoche wiederbelebt, es muss immer auch

poutres de bois, des sols en pierres ou en dalles de terre cuite, des meubles simples et fonctionnels et des objets décoratifs rappelant les cuisines campagnardes : marmites, théières, carafes antiques, fruits et fleures des champs disposés dan des paniers, des bouquets d'herbes mis à sécher et des ustensiles de fer suspendus à la cheminée prêts à l'emploi.

Les cuisines classiques représentent une autre option de décoration. Elles sont d'un style éclectique et se distinguent de par leur élégance, leur confort et un mobilier de grande qualité. Avec des lignes raffinées et une décoration purement bourgeoise elles créent une ambiance d'époque. On peut parfois retrouver une atmosphère que classique en ajoutant des pièces de cette époque, en atténuant la lumière et disposant un mobilier simple de manière élégante.

conseguirse en tiendas de almoneda o rastros o bien restaurando, barnizando, encerando o decapando un mueble antiguo de herencia para darle un nuevo uso. El estilo rústico se define por techos de vigas de madera y suelos de piedra o baldosas de barro cocido, muebles simples y muy funcionales con objetos decorativos que recuerdan las cocinas antiguas del campo: ollas, teteras o jarras antiguas, frutas, flores silvestres en cestos o manojos de hierbas colgados a secar. Y en la chimenea, útiles de hierro para su funcionamiento.

Las cocinas clásicas son otra opción decorativa. Se trata de un estilo ecléctico que destaca por la suma de elegancia, confort y mobiliario de gran calidad. Se trata de un estilo que recrea un ambiente de época, con formas refinadas y una decoración puramente burguesa. A veces puede conseguirse una ambientación

classical ambience can be granted by placing a few pieces from the period, making use of subdued lighting or using simple furniture placed with elegance. Apart from evoking the period, it is essential that the furniture be practical and functional. The use of wood on the walls and floor is another good option. The walls can be paneled with wood and framed with mouldings or strips of pinewood, which have been applied decorative tecniques that imitate a marble design, like that used in the baroque style. Classical ceiling mouldings with floral designs can be combined with cornices and columns. Large glass cabinets, chests of drawers and shelves are

funktionell sein. Holz ist eine gute Wahl für Wände und Fußböden. Die Wände können mit durch Kieferprofilleisten umrandeten Holzpaneelen verkleidet werden, die zusätzlich mit Dekorationstechniken wie der im Barock beliebten Marmorimitation verziert sind. Möglichkeiten der Deckendekoration sind klassische Zierleisten mit Blumenmotiven oder Girlanden, kombiniert mit Gesims und Säulen. Zu geeigneten Möbeln in klassischem Stil gehören große Vitrinen, Kommoden und Regale. Die Kombination von Möbeln aus unterschiedlichen klassischen Epochen ist ohne Weiteres möglich, solange sie eines gemeinsam haben: Eleganz.

Der moderne Stil tendiert dazu, alle Wohnbereiche zu vereinheitlichen und zu integrieren, dabei jedoch stets ihre Intimität zu bewahren, um so flexible, an ihre jeweilige Funktion angepasste Räume

Dans la cuisine il et important que les meubles non seulement évoquent une certaine période, mais soient pratiques et fonctionnels. Le bois pour le sol et les parois est une bonne option. On peut revêtir les parois de panneaux de bois et les encadrer de moulures ou de lamelles de pins et en appliquant certaines techniques de décoration imitant le marbre très utilisé pour le baroque. Les plafonds pouvant avoir des moulures classiques avec des motifs floraux ou des guirlandes ainsi que des corniches et des colonnes. Les meubles de design classiques conseillés pour la cuisine sont de grandes vitrines, des commodes et des

clásica colocando algunas piezas que recreen la época, utilizando una iluminación tenue o un mobiliario sencillo dispuesto con elegancia. En la cocina es imprescindible que el mobiliario, además de inspirar la época, sea práctico y muy funcional. La madera para las paredes y suelos es una buena opción. Las paredes pueden revestirse con paneles de madera, enmarcados con molduras o bien con listones de pino, aplicándoles alguna técnica decorativa como la que imita el mármol, que se utilizaba mucho en el barroco. Los techos pueden incorporar molduras clásicas, con motivos florales o guirnaldas, a juego con cornisas

examples of classical design furniture, which is appropriated for the kitchen. Styles may be mixed. As long as the furniture is elegant, furniture reminiscent of different periods can be used together.

Modern style tends to unify and integrate each space while at the same time allowing it to maintain its privacy. It attempts to afford flexible spaces yet well adapted to their use. New architectural concepts inspire contemporary interior decoration. New tendencies include

zu schaffen. Ausgangspunkt einer Ausstattung sind heute neue architektonische Konzepte, die hin zu großen Räumen ohne Trennwände gehen. Der Loft, normalerweise industriell genutzt, setzt auf die Schaffung offener multifunktionaler Räume. Bei dieser Tendenz steht die Bequemlichkeit im Vordergrund. Die Küche wird nunmehr zum Mehrzweckraum mit Gemeinschaftszonen für die Familie, mit Bereichen für das ungezwungene Beisammensein mit Freunden

étagères. Une combinaison de meubles d'époques différentes est toujours très élégante.

Le style moderne tend à unifier chacun des espaces et à les intégrer tout en respectant l'intimité de chacun d'entre eux. Afin de créer un espace flexible et adapté à chaque usage. La décoration actuelle surgit de conceptions architecturales nouvelles. Les grands espaces sans cloisons de séparation, représentent les nouvelles tendances. Le concept du loft, émergeant d'un concept industriel crée des espaces ouverts et à fonctions multiples. Il s'agit d'une tendance ou le confort est primordial. La cuisine est un espace à fonctions multiples destiné à la famille, à se réunir avec des amis ou destiné uniquement à la préparation des repas. Les meubles sont plus légers et flexibles et beaucoup d'entre eux peuvent être déplacés facilement.

y columnas. Los muebles de diseño clásico adecuados para la cocina son grandes vitrinas, cómodas y estanterías. Pueden mezclarse muebles inspirados en diversas épocas clásicas, siempre que sean elegantes.

El estilo moderno tiende a unificar cada uno de los espacios e integrarlos, respetando siempre la intimidad de cada uno de ellos, para lograr un espacio flexible y adaptado a sus usos. La decoración actual surge a partir de nuevas concepciones arquitectónicas. Los grandes espacios sin tabiques divisorios constituyen las nuevas tendencias. El concepto de loft, normalmente de concepción industrial, apuesta por crear espacios abiertos de múltiples funciones. Se trata de una tendencia en la que prima la comodidad. La cocina es ahora un espacio de múltiples funciones, con ambientes comunes destinados a la familia o a las

large spaces without dividing partitions. The loft concept, emerging from an industrial concept, entails designing open spaces for multiple uses. This tendency places comfort at the forefront. Nowadays, the kitchen is a space for multiple uses where there are spaces for the family or for meeting with friends, and spaces exclusively for food preparation. The furniture is light, flexible and easily movable. Generally, contemporary decoration is eclectic. Nothing is taboo; the most important thing is to design a comfortable and practical space, which is directly related to the use for which it is designed. This is based on the needs of the users. Depending on whether it is for one individual or a large family, for a person who never cooks or one who enjoys trying out recipes, the design will vary. When choosing furniture, it is not only a question of opting for the latest design

oder für die Zubereitung der Mahlzeiten. Die leichteren und flexibleren Möbel können zum Teil mühelos verschoben werden. Im Allgemeinen ist die Ausstattung heute eklektisch: Nichts ist verboten. Wichtig ist nur die Gestaltung eines bequemen und praktischen Raumes, der in direkter Beziehung zu seiner jeweiligen Nutzung steht. Grundlage sind die ureigensten Bedürfnisse seiner Benutzer. Das Design einer Küche wird variiert, je nach dem, ob sie für eine Einzelperson oder eine Großfamilie, für jemanden, der niemals kocht, oder für einen Hobbykoch, der Freude am Ausprobieren neuer Rezepte hat, vorgesehen ist. Möbel für eine zeitgenössische Ausstattung auszuwählen, heißt nicht unbedingt, Einrichtungsstücke von hochaktuellem Design zu erwerben. Es können auch ältere Stücke verwendet und dem Zeitgeist angepasst, in einer anderen Farbe

En général la décoration actuelle est éclectique : rien n'est interdit, l'important étant de concevoir un espace commode et pratique et directement relié à l'usage que l'on veut en faire. Elle est basée sur les nécessités propres de l'usager, changeant si elle est destinée à un individu unique, une famille nombreuse, une personne ne faisant jamais la cuisine ou quelqu'un qui aime essayer de nouvelles recettes. Choisir des meubles pour une décoration contemporaine ne signifie pas uniquement acquérir des meubles de design actuel. On peut utiliser des pièces antiques en les actualisant, en les peignant d'une autre couleur ou en leur donnant un nouvel usage. Les meubles de cuisine actuels ont des lignes droites et simples, peuvent être employés de façons multiples et sont faciles à transporter. Les matériaux les plus utilisés sont ceux qui ajoutent de la

reuniones con los amigos y espacios únicamente para la elaboración de la comida. Los muebles son más ligeros y flexibles y algunos de ellos pueden desplazarse fácilmente. En general, la decoración actual es ecléctica: no hay nada prohibido, lo más importante es concebir un espacio cómodo y práctico, y esto está directamente relacionado con el uso que se haga de él: se basa en las necesidades propias de sus usuarios. La cocina cambia si se proyecta para un único individuo o una familia numerosa, para una persona que nunca cocina o para quien disfruta probando nuevas recetas. Elegir muebles para una decoración contemporánea no se traduce únicamente en adquirir muebles de último diseño. Pueden utilizarse piezas antiguas actualizándolas, pintándolas de otro color o dándoles un nuevo uso. Los muebles actuales en la cocina son de

furniture. Old pieces can be updated by painting them another color or using them in another way. Contemporary kitchen furniture has straight, simple lines, is designed for multiple-use and easily movable. The most commonly used materials are those which afford lightness, like glass, and a natural touch, like wood or natural fibers.

The latest tendencies incorporate large spaces, which pay tribute to oriental traditions. They are clean, simple spaces with a pure Zen aesthetic. They are laid out following the guidelines of millenari-un traditions such as feng shui, which improves the layout of each space.

gestrichen oder umfunktioniert werden. Aktuelle Küchenmöbel haben gerade und einfache Linien, können vielseitig eingesetzt werden und sind leicht zu transportieren. Die am häufigsten anzu-treffenden Materialien sind jene, die ih-nen Leichtigkeit – wie z. B. Glas – oder einen Hauch von Natürlichkeit – wie Holz und Naturfasern – verleihen.

Die neuen Trends setzen auf weite Räume und stellen eine Reverenz an orientalische Traditionen dar: an den rei-nen Zen-Stil mit klaren und schlichten Räumen, die nach den Regeln jahrtau-sendealter Traditionen wie dem Feng-Shui angeordnet werden, um so die Ge-staltung eines jeden Raumes zu verbessern.

légèreté comme le verre ou une touche naturelle comme le bois ou les fibres naturelles.

Les tendances actuelles plaident pour de grands espaces rendant hommage aux traditions orientales, de pure esthétique zen avec des espaces nets et simples répartis en suivant des traditions millénaires comme le Feng Shui, qui améliore la configuration de chaque espace.

líneas rectas y simples, dotados de múltiples usos y fácilmente transportables. Los materiales más utilizados son aquellos que añaden ligereza, como el cristal, y que aportan un toque natural, como la madera o las fibras naturales.

Las nuevas tendencias abogan por amplios espacios que rinden homenaje a tradiciones orientales, de pura estética zen con espacios limpios y simples, distribuidos siguiendo los consejos de tradiciones milenarias como el feng shui, que mejora la configuración de cada espacio.

ASPECTS

Aspects
du design
Aspekte
des Designs

OF DESIGN

*Aspectos
de diseño*

KITCHEN LAYOUT

The latest kitchens are being designed as spacious rooms, which facilitate the preparation and cooking of food, afford sufficient storage space and allow for a space where meals can be enjoyed. They commonly reserve a space for the so-called "office". Before deciding on a distribution, it is advisable to clarify your priorites and decide how the furniture will be arranged, bearing in mind the space available. In this respect, then it is important to establish the three main zones of the kitchen: the water zone (the sink), the cooking zone (the range) and the food storage zone. Put in another way, the place where the food will be cleaned and prepared, where it will be cooked and where it will be stored. The key lies in setting up an imaginary triangle between the three zones so that they are close, but kept at a certain distance so that the tasks do not bump into each other. Each zone should function as an independent unit while at the same time, be communicated with the others, so as to facilitate the work. The ideal arrangement is that each zone includes storage space for its own utensils and the food. The starting point for the distribution is the sink, which can be installed under a window or in a work island. Next to it, though separated by a counter (depending on the distribution, even situated in front), the range with the oven, the microwave oven and the other appliances, can be installed. Then, there is the area with the refrigerator and the pantries for storing food. Once the "triangle" distribution has been decided, the placement of the other accessories is an easy task. Depending on the space available, different types of distribution are possible. A linear kitchen lines up the cabinets on a wall, which is the ideal design, when the kitchen is small and elongated. It is common to situate two parallel rows of cabinets, one high up on the wall and the other low on the floor. An L-shaped arrangement is used when there are two adjacent walls. It is very useful as it allows the installation of many cabinets and drawers while at the same time providing an open, uncluttered central space. A U-shaped distribution allows three walls to be used which affords an uninterrupted space for preparing food. In large square kitchens, a distribution with a central island lets you work very conveniently and comfortably. Some of the main parts of the kitchen can be centralized here, such as the sink or the cooking area.

AUFTEILUNG DER KÜCHE

Die neuen Küchen werden als großzügige Räume entworfen, um die Vorbereitungen und Essenszubereitung zu erleichtern, über genügend Aufbewahrungskapazitäten zu verfügen und das Essen genießen zu können, indem man Platz für eine Essecke mit einplant. Bevor man die Aufteilung festlegt, ist es wichtig, sich über die Prioritäten in jedem Einzelfall Gedanken zu machen und die Möbelverteilung je nach Raumangebot zu entscheiden. Dafür ist es wichtig, die Küche als erstes in drei Bereiche aufzuteilen: den Nassbereich (Spüle), den Kochbereich (Herd) und den Aufbewahrungsbereich (Speisen). Anders gesagt: zu entscheiden, wo die Speisen gewaschen und vorbereitet, wo sie gekocht und wo sie aufbewahrt werden. Für die optimale Lösung denkt man sich am besten ein Dreieck zwischen diesen drei Bereichen, in dem sie einander zwar nahe liegen, jedoch ein gewisser Platzabstand zwischen ihnen besteht, damit die verschiedenen Arbeitsprozesse nicht miteinander kollidieren. Um die Arbeit zu erleichtern, sollte jeder als unabhängiger Bereich funktionieren, der aber mit den anderen verbunden ist. Ideal wäre es, wenn in jeder dieser Zonen Platz für die jeweiligen Utensilien und Lebensmittel ist. Ausgangspunkt der Aufteilung ist die Spüle, welche sich unter einem Fenster oder in einer Arbeitsinsel einbauen lässt. Anschließend, wenn auch getrennt durch eine Arbeitsfläche (welche auch gegenüberliegend untergebracht werden kann, je nach der gewählten Aufteilung), kann man den Kochbereich mit Ofen, Mikrowellenherd und den sonstigen Elektrogeräten platzieren. Danach folgt der Aufbewahrungsbereich mit Kühlschrank und Schränken zur Lagerung der Lebensmittel. Wenn einmal dieses „Aufteilungsdreieck" erstellt wurde, erweist sich die Anordnung des weiteren Zubehörs als einfach. Je nach verfügbarem Platz sind unterschiedliche Arten der Aufteilung möglich. Die geradlinige Küchenzeile, welche die Schränke in einer Linie und an einer Wand aufreiht, ist sehr günstig bei kleinen und länglichen Küchen. Meist lassen sich zwei parallele Schrankreihen (Hängeschränke und Unterschränke) anbringen. Die Gestaltung in L-Form benützt zwei zusammenhängende Wände und ist sehr praktisch, nicht nur durch die große Anzahl von Schränken und Schubladen, welche man in ihr unterbringen kann, sondern auch durch den freien Platz, der in der Mitte entsteht. Die Aufteilung in U-Form erlaubt es drei Wände zu nutzen, und stellt eine zusammenhängende Fläche für die Zubereitung zur Verfügung. Bei großen, quadratischen Küchen ermöglicht eine Arbeitsinsel eine sehr bequeme Arbeitsweise. In einer solchen Insel kann man Teile der Grundausstattung einer Küche, wie die Spüle oder den Kochbereich zentral unterbringen.

L'AGENCEMENT DE LA CUISINE

Les nouvelles cuisines sont conçues comme des pièces vastes, facilitant la préparation et la cuisson des aliments, disposant d'un endroit pour les stocker, d'une place pour jouir des repas ainsi que d'une zone tenant lieu d'office. Avant de décider de l'agencement, il est sage de penser à ses priorités et de décider de l'emplacement des meubles en fonction de l'espace disponible. De ce fait il est important de définir dès le départ les trois zones principales de la cuisine: La zone de l'eau (l'évier), celle où l'on cuit (les fourneaux) et celle destinée au rangement. C'est à dire: l'endroit où on lave et où on prépare la nourriture, l'endroit où on la cuit et celui où elle est emmagasinée. La meilleure solution et de penser à un triangle imaginaire entre ces zones afin qu'elles soient proches l'une de l'autre tout en gardant une certaine distance pour éviter un mélange des différentes tâches. Chaque partie de la cuisine devant fonctionner comme unité indépendante tout en communiquant avec les autres pour faciliter le travail. L'idéal serait que chacune de ces zones ait une place propre pour ranger les ustensiles et la nourriture que l'on y emploie. Le point de départ pour effectuer la répartition est l'évier, qui peut être installé sous une fenêtre ou intégré à une île de travail. Ensuite, tout en étant séparé par un plan de travail (ou en face selon le choix de la répartition) on peut installer la cuisinière, le four, les micro-ondes et d'autres appareils électro-ménagers. Enfin, la partie de rangement comprenant le frigidaire ainsi que les armoires pour garder les aliments. Ayant conçu ce triangle, il est facile de placer les autres accessoires. Dépendant de la place disponible, l'agencement peut se faire de différentes façons. Pur une cuisine petite et allongée, la meilleure solution est une rangée d'armoires placée le long de la paroi, comprenant une rangée d'armoires suspendues et une rangée au sol. Ayant deux parois adjacentes on peut concevoir une cuisine en forme de L, permettant de placer de nombreuses armoires tout en gardant un espace libre au centre. Un agencement en forme de U permet d'utiliser trois parois et d'avoir un espace ininterrompu pour travailler. Dans une grande cuisine carrée, une île de travail centrale s'avère très pratique. On peut y intégrer le plus important, c'est à dire l'évier et la cuisinière.

DISTRIBUCIÓN DE LA COCINA

Las nuevas cocinas se proyectan como amplias estancias para facilitar la preparación y elaboración de los alimentos, disponer de suficiente capacidad para el almacenamiento y para disfrutar de las comidas, reservando una zona para el office. Antes de decidir la distribución, es conveniente planificar las prioridades de cada caso particular y decidir cómo va a colocarse el mobiliario en función del espacio disponible. Para ello, es importante establecer una primera separación de las tres principales zonas de la cocina: la zona de aguas (el fregadero), la de cocción (los fogones) y la parte destinada al almacenamiento, o lo que es lo mismo: decidir la zona donde se lavan y preparan los alimentos, donde se cocinan y el lugar donde se guardan. La clave consiste en establecer un triángulo imaginario entre estas zonas, de forma que estén cerca, aunque a cierta distancia para no mezclar las tareas. Cada una de las partes de la cocina debe funcionar como unidad independiente, aunque comunicada con las demás para facilitar el trabajo. Lo ideal sería que cada una de las partes integrara un espacio propio para almacenar el menaje y los alimentos. El punto de partida de la distribución es el fregadero, que puede instalarse debajo de una ventana o en una isla de trabajo. A continuación, aunque separada por la encimera, (o bien enfrente, en función de la distribución elegida), puede situarse la cocina con el horno, el microondas y los demás electrodomésticos. Y a continuación, la zona de almacén con la nevera y armarios para guardar todos los alimentos. Una vez decidido "el triángulo" de distribución, la colocación de los otros accesorios resulta tarea fácil. Se establecen varios tipos de distribución, en función del espacio disponible. La cocina lineal incorpora los armarios alineados contra una pared, planificación muy útil cuando la cocina es reducida y alargada. En ella pueden disponerse dos filas de armarios paralelos (superiores e inferiores). La configuración en forma de L equipa dos paredes adyacentes. Resulta muy útil porque permite situar gran cantidad de armarios y cajones, además de proporcionar un espacio central abierto y despejado. La distribución en forma de U es la que permite aprovechar tres paredes, proporcionando un espacio ininterrumpido para la preparación de los alimentos. En cocinas amplias y cuadradas, la distribución de una isla central permite poder trabajar de forma muy cómoda. En ella pueden centralizarse algunas de las partes básicas de la cocina, como el fregadero o la zona de cocción.

FURNITURE

Storage space for utensils and food should be planned around the three main distribution zones: the sink, the cooking zone and the pantry. It is best to store the most commonly used utensils in the most accessible way and those, which are only occasionally used, tucked away in the back and far away. Classic designs in the work area include upper and lower cabinets in order to take maximum advantage of the space available. New contemporary designs using large drawers with multiple compartments are replacing cabinets with doors. This type of furniture offers an extensive variety of practical modules for each kitchen zone. The pull-out drawers with big handles for large pots are a good option for keeping the pots in order next to the cooking area. The silverware drawers include trays for organizing the silverware and other items such as spice trays and small appliances. There are also pull-out modules for storing lids and plates, which can be installed near the water zone or the dishwasher. You can also find specialized cabinets with ingenious arrangements for cleaning products. There are modules with revolving axis and pull-out baskets or drawers, which take maximum advantage of the space of any corner. The latest modules use trays, dividing boxes, stainless steel extendible grates, to divide up and maximize the use of their interior space. For the pantry, full-height high capacity cabinets are in vogue. The majority employ rails and slide out trays, which let you easily, open and close the drawers. Some even include bottle racks or small independent boxes for stowing away small packages. Pull-out drawers for storing the least used items may even be found situated behind the moldings. The majority of kitchens combine drawers and closed modules with glass cabinets or shelves, which leave dishes or other items in view. If this is your choice, then it is of utmost importance to always have the area in view, neat. The least attractive objects can be concealed behind closed doors. Bars and racks are practical, complementary, kitchen furnishings. Whether hung from the wall over the counter or even hanging from the ceiling, they can prove both decorative and practical.

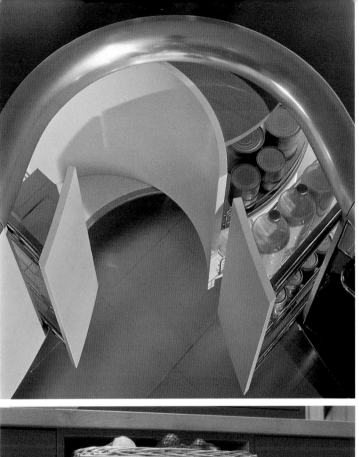

MÖBLIERUNG

Der für die Lagerung und Aufbewahrung der Utensilien und Lebensmittel gedachte Platz sollte rund um die drei grundlegenden Bereiche geplant werden: um die Spüle, den Kochbereich und den eigentlichen Speiseschrank. Am besten bringt man die Gegenstände, welche am meisten gebraucht werden, in den erreichbareren Bereichen unter (nahe an den Arbeitsflächen) und Gegenstände, die man nur gelegentlich zur Hand nimmt, in den tieferen Teilen der Schränke. Die traditionelle Küche sieht Ober- und Unterschränke vor, um so den Platz auch unter den Arbeitsflächen optimal auszunützen. Zur Zeit werden im neuen Küchenmöbeldesign Schränke mit Türen durch große Schubladen mit vielfältigen zusätzlichen Unterteilungen ersetzt. Auf diesem Möbeltyp basiert eine Vielzahl von praktischen Modulen für jeden Küchenbereich. Herausnehmbare Topfschubladen mit großen Griffen bieten die Möglichkeit, das Kochtopf-Set ordentlich in der Nähe des Kochbereichs unterzubringen. Die Besteckschubläden haben Einlagetabletts für das Besteck und andere nützliche Dinge, wie Gewürzständer und kleine Elektrogeräte. Es existieren auch herausnehmbare Module für das Aufbewahren von Tellern und Deckeln, welche sich in der Nähe der Spüle und des Geschirrspülers unterbringen lassen, oder auch raffinierte Schränke für Reinigungsmittel. Um alle Ecken auszunützen, gibt es Module mit drehbaren Achsen, oder herausnehmbare Körbchen und Kästchen. Neue Modelle verfügen in ihrem Inneren über Tabletts, Trennwände oder auch herausziehbare Gitterunterlagen aus rostfreiem Stahl, um den Innenraum aufzuteilen und optimal zu nutzen. Als Speiseschrank werden Säulenschränke mit großer Lagerkapazität verwandt. Die meisten von ihnen laufen auf Schienen, um ein reibungsloses Öffnen und Schließen der Schubladen zu gewährleisten. Es gibt besondere Modelle mit Flaschenständern oder für die Lagerung von Kleinstteilen. In die Küchensockel können herausnehmbare Schubladen eingebaut werden, in denen das selten benützte Zubehör untergebracht werden kann. Die meisten Küchen kombinieren Schubläden und geschlossene Module mit Vitrinen und Regalen, so dass Geschirr und andere Elemente teilweise sichtbar sind. Wenn man sich dafür entscheidet, ist es allerdings unabdingbar, diese Bereiche immer in Ordnung zu halten. Nicht so attraktive Objekte kann man hinter geschlossenen Türen verstecken. Stangen und Schienen sind praktische Zubehörteile für Küchenmöbel. An der Küchenfront angebracht oder von der Decke hängend können sie sowohl nützlich als auch dekorativ sein.

LE MOBILIER

Il est indispensable de planifier des places de rangement pour les ustensiles et la nourriture dans chacune des trois zones: évier, fourneaux et office, plaçant les ustensiles employés plus fréquemment à l'avant et les autres d'utilisation moins fréquente à l'arrière. Le design classique prévoit des modules pour la partie supérieure et la partie Inférieure, afin de pouvoir employer au maximum la place mise à disposition. Le design contemporain remplace les portes par de grands tiroirs à compartiments multiples. Ce type de meuble offre une grande variété d'éléments très pratiques pouvant être adaptés à chaque cuisine. Ces tiroirs aux larges poignées offrent une possibilité de rangement idéale pour la batterie de cuisine à proximité des fourneaux. D'autres tiroirs sont destinés aux services, aux épices ainsi qu'à d'autres ustensiles et électro-ménagers de petite taille. Il en existe également pour ranger les couvercles et la vaisselle, ceux-ci devant être placés dans la zone « eau », à proximité du lave-vaisselle. On trouve aussi des armoires ingénieuses destinées au rangement des produits de nettoyage, et celles à portes, tiroirs ou corbeilles tournantes permettant d'utiliser au maximum chaque recoin. Les plus modernes ayant des subdivisions métalliques amovibles ou des bases pivotantes pour délimiter les espaces intérieurs. Les armoires réservées aux aliment sont des armoires hautes ayant une grande capacité de rangement. La pluspart sont sur rails, permettant de les ouvrir et de les fermer facilement. Certains modèles ont des compartiments pour les bouteilles ou permettant de ranger les choses les plus petites. On peut également installer des tiroirs dans les socles, dans lesquels on pourra mettre les accessoires les moins employés. La majorité des cuisines combinent des tiroirs à des vitrines fermées, permettant de voir la vaisselle ou d'autres objets exposés. Choisissant cette option on est obligé de les maintenir toujours en ordre. Les choses les moins attrayantes pouvant être dissimulées derrière des portes fermées. Des barres et des rails sont très pratiques. Fixés aux parois, au dessus du plan de travail ou au plafond, ils peuvent être des éléments très utiles et décoratifs de la cuisine.

MOBILIARIO

El espacio dedicado a almacenar los utensilios y alimentos debe planificarse alrededor de las tres zonas principales de distribución: la del fregadero, la de cocción y la propia despensa. Lo más útil es colocar el menaje que más se utiliza en las partes más accesibles (cerca de las áreas de trabajo) y los utensilios que se usan sólo de forma ocasional en la zona más profunda de los armarios. Los diseños clásicos incorporan módulos en la zona superior e inferior de la zona de trabajo para aprovechar al máximo las dimensiones de la cocina. En la actualidad, los nuevos diseños de muebles para la cocina sustituyen los armarios de puertas por cajones de grandes dimensiones con múltiples subdivisiones. Este tipo de mobiliario ofrece una extensa variedad de módulos prácticos creados para cada zona de la cocina. Los cajones caceroleros extraíbles con grandes tiradores son una buena opción para tener bien ordenada la batería de cocina, junto a la zona de cocción. Los cajones cuberteros disponen de bandejas organizadoras para cubiertos y otros útiles, como especieros y pequeños electrodomésticos. También existen módulos extraíbles para guardar tapas y platos, que pueden colocarse cerca de la zona de aguas y el lavavajillas, o ingeniosos armarios para los productos de limpieza. Para aprovechar al máximo los rincones existen módulos con ejes giratorios o cestas y cajones extraíbles. Los nuevos módulos utilizan en su interior bandejas, cajones divisores o parrillas extensibles de acero inoxidable para delimitar el espacio interior. Para la zona de la despensa se utilizan columnas de armarios de gran capacidad. La mayoría de ellas utilizan rieles que abren y cierran los cajones fácilmente. Algunos modelos incluso incorporan armarios que albergan botelleros en su interior, o pequeñas cajas independientes para almacenar los paquetes más pequeños. Los zócalos de la cocina pueden incorporar cajones extraíbles que permiten almacenar los accesorios que menos se utilicen. La mayoría de cocinas combinan cajones y módulos cerrados con vitrinas o estanterías que dejan a la vista vajillas u otros elementos. Si se opta por esta combinación, es imprescindible tener siempre ordenada la zona más visible. Los objetos menos atractivos pueden ocultarse tras las puertas cerradas. Las barras y rieles son prácticos complementos para el mobiliario de la cocina. Situados en el antepecho de la cocina o incluso suspendidos en el techo, resultan elementos muy prácticos y decorativos.

73

MATERIALS AND COVERINGS

Just as in the bathroom, a careful choice of the materials to be used for the coverings is very important, as the style of the decoration depends on this choice. You must bear in mind the appearance and color but the selection must also be based on the material's ability to withstand humidity and changes of temperature. Likewise, ease of cleaning is very important. Nowadays, all types of flooring, cabinets and counters are available which are both durable and practical, and adapt to any type of decoration or space. Apart from being indispensable for storing kitchen items and food, the cabinets are also aesthetically important in the kitchen. The wide range of materials available does not facilitate the choice, which will depend on the style and priorities of the users. With such a variety of tones, a wood finish is a good option. The lightest tones such as pine, maple, birch and beech make the space seem larger whereas the darker varieties such as the tropical woods (iroko and wengué, especially) grant greater elegance. Wood, being a porous and absorbent material, needs to be specially treated so that it can withstand steam and splashing. As a general rule, the cabinets are not made of solid wood, but rather, different types of plywood: a particle board base over which is applied a layer of fine wood. There is the lacquered-type finish, which uses lacquer or varnish for covering a particle board base. It is very durable and available in a wide-variety of colors. Synthetic resin laminates are another option, which prove very resistant to gashes and scratching. At present, steel modules are in vogue. They are very durable and easy to clean. Just like the laminated materials, wood treated with varnish, natural oils or resins, it is also used for the counters. Marble is another material commonly used in the work area of the kitchen. It is durable though especially vulnerable to acids and abrasive detergents. Granite, which does not stain nor scratch and is not affected by changes in temperature, is another very appropriate natural stone. At present, a wide variety of synthetic counters are available. Ir'O, Corian or Silestone, which bear the names of their manufacturers are materials which consist of natural minerals and resins, and they adapt to any type of surface. The latest generation of kitchen ranges has opted for materials such as high-temperature heat-resistant glass, and methacrylate. Kitchen floors must be very resistant to staining and afford ease of cleaning. Stoneware does not easily show the dirt and is easy to maintain. Silestone and other synthetic materials are resistant and come in a wide variety of colors. Marble embellishes the surroundings though it must be treated regularly. Synthetic parquet is also a very fine option.

MATERIALIEN UND WANDGESTALTUNGEN

Die Wandgestaltung ist in der Küche genauso wie im Badezimmer sehr wichtig, da sie den Stil des Raumes prägen. Man muss bei der Materialwahl außer auf Farbe und Aussehen auch auf die Widerstandsfähigkeit gegen Feuchtigkeit, Temperaturschwankungen und die Pflegeleichtigkeit achten. Böden, Schränke und Arbeitsplatten werden in vielfältigen, praktischen Materialien hergestellt, die an sämtliche Raumverhältnisse und jeden Dekorationsstil angepasst werden können. Schränke sind nicht nur unverzichtbarer Aufbewahrungsort für Utensilien und Lebensmittel, sondern auch ästhetisches Stilmittel. Die Materialvielfalt macht die Auswahl nicht gerade leicht, die von Stil und Prioritäten des Benutzers abhängt. Ausfertigungen aus Holz bieten durch eine große Farbpalette und Holzarten eine bedenkenswerte Auswahl. Hellere Hölzer wie Pinie, Birke, Buche oder auch Ahorn scheinen den Raum zu vergrößern, während dunklere Holzsorten, wie z. B. Tropenhölzer (besonders Iroko und Wengué) der Küche mehr Eleganz verleihen. Da Holz eine poröse Oberfläche hat, benötigt es eine spezielle Behandlung, um Wasserdampf und Spritzwasser zu widerstehen. Im allgemeinen werden Küchenschränke nicht in Massivholz, sondern mit Furnier hergestellt, das heißt auf Pressspanplatten wird eine Schicht hochwertiges Holz aufgeklebt. Lackoberflächen, bei denen Lack oder Firnis die Basis aus Pressplatten schützt, stellen eine Alternative dar. Sie sind widerstandsfähig und in einer großen Farbvielfalt erhältlich. Aus synthetischen Harzen hergestellte Laminate sind ebenfalls strapazierfähig und halten Stöße und Kratzer aus. Stahlmodule sind zur Zeit sehr in Mode: Sie sind sehr hart und leicht zu reinigen. Darum setzt man dieses Material auch für Arbeitsplatten ein, genauso wie Laminate und mit natürlichen Ölen, Harzen und Firnis behandelte Hölzer. Marmor wird auch häufig für den Arbeitsbereich verwendet. Er ist widerstandsfähig, jedoch anfällig gegenüber Säure und scharfen Reinigungsmitteln. Ein anderer geeigneter Naturstein ist Granit, da er weder verschmutzt noch zerkratzt werden kann sowie Temperaturschwankungen aushält. Heutzutage existiert eine Vielfalt an synthetisch hergestellten Arbeitsplatten die den Namen des Fabrikanten tragen, wie zum Beispiel Ir'O, Corian oder Silestone: Materialien aus natürlichen Mineralien und Harzen, die sich an jegliche Oberfläche anpassen lassen. Küchen der neuesten Generation werden auch mit Verbundglas oder Metaakrylat gestaltet. Der Boden einer Küche muss äußerst widerstandsfähig gegenüber Flecken und leicht zu reinigen sein. Steingut ist ein Material, das belastungsfähig und pflegeleicht ist; Silestone und andere synthetische Materialien sind strapazierfähig und bieten eine weitreichende Farbpalette; Holz und Marmor sind zwar sehr dekorativ, müssen aber regelmäßig behandelt werden. Ebenfalls gut in der Küche einzusetzen ist synthetischer Parkettboden.

MATÉRIAUX ET REVÊTEMENTS

Le choix des revêtements employés dans la cuisine est aussi important que pour la salle de bains, le style de décoration en dépendant. Le choix des matériaux devant tenir compte de l'apparence et de la couleur, de la résistance à l'humidité et aux changements de températures ainsi que de la facilité à les nettoyer. De nos jours on trouve des matériaux résistants et pratiques, s'adaptant à tous les types d'espace et de décoration. Les armoires sont non seulement indispensables au rangement des articles de ménage et de la nourriture, mais constituent un élément esthétique important dans la cuisine. La diversité des matériaux offerts sur le marché ne facilitant pas le choix, dont pourtant dépend le style et les priorités de l'usager. Les finitions en bois offrant une gamme de variétés et de tons différents sont une bonne option. Les bois clairs tels que le pin, l'érable, le bouleau et le hêtre paraissent visuellement agrandir l'espace tandis que les bois foncés et tropicaux (l'iroco et le wengué particulièrement) lui confère une grande élégance. Étant un matériel poreux et absorbant, le bois nécessite un traitement spécial afin de résister à la vapeur et aux éclaboussures. Les armoires de cuisine ne sont généralement pas construites en bois massif mais en contre-plaqué (des copeaux de bois agglomérés et recouvert d'une couche de bois noble). Une autre possibilité étant de les peindre avec une laque ou un vernis pour protéger le aggloméré. Cela en fait un matériel résistant et que l'on peut obtenir dans une grande variété de couleurs. Le contre-plaqué à base de résines synthétiques est également très résistant aux coups et aux rayures. Les modules en acier sont très en vogue en ce moment. Ils sont résistants et faciles à nettoyer. C'est pourquoi on l'emploie aussi pour les comptoirs de même que les contre-plaqués et les bois traités aux vernis, aux huiles naturelles ou résines. Le marbre est employé fréquemment pour les plans de travail. Il est résistant bien que vulnérable aux acides et aux détergents. Une autre pierre naturelle et adéquate est le granit qui ne se tache pas, ne se raie pas et est inaltérable aux changements de température. Il existe en outre un choix de comptoirs synthétiques comme par exemple le Ir'O, le Corian ou le Silestone; matériaux composés de minéraux naturels et de résines pouvant s'adapter à n'importe quelle superficie. Les cuisines de la nouvelle génération misent sur des matériaux tels que le verre blindé et méthacrylique. Le sol d'une cuisine doit être très résistant aux taches et facile à nettoyer. Sur le grès on ne voit guère la saleté et il est d'un entretien facile. Le Silestone et les matériaux synthétiques sont très résistants et on peut les obtenir dans un grand choix de couleurs. Le bois et le marbre embellissent les pourtours mais doivent être traités régulièrement. Les parquets synthétiques sont également une bonne solution.

MATERIALES Y REVESTIMIENTOS

La elección de los revestimientos utilizados en la cocina, al igual que en el cuarto del baño, es muy importante, puesto que de ello depende su estilo decorativo. Además de por su apariencia y color, los materiales deben elegirse en función de la resistencia a la humedad, a los cambios de temperatura y a su facilidad de limpieza. Suelos, armarios y encimeras ofrecen múltiples materiales resistentes y prácticos que se adaptan a cualquier espacio y decoración. Los armarios, además de ser imprescindibles para guardar el menaje y los alimentos, constituyen un importante elemento estético en la cocina. La amplia gama de materiales que ofrece el mercado no facilita la elección, y de ello depende el estilo y las prioridades de los usuarios. Los acabados de madera son una buena opción y, además, ofrecen una gran gama de tonos y variedades. Los más claros como el pino, el arce, el abedul y el haya parecen ampliar visualmente el espacio, mientras que sus variedades más oscuras, como las maderas tropicales (iroco y wengué especialmente), dan mayor elegancia. La madera, un material poroso y absorbente, requiere de un tratamiento especial para que pueda resistir el vapor de agua y las salpicaduras. Generalmente los armarios de cocina no se realizan con madera maciza sino con chapados: una base de conglomerado a la que se añade una lámina de madera noble. Otro tipo de acabado es el lacado, con barniz o laca que protege una base de conglomerado. Se trata de un material resistente, comercializado con una extensa variedad de colores. Los laminados, realizados con resinas sintéticas, son otra opción resistente a los golpes y a las rayaduras. Los módulos de acero resultan muy actuales: presentan una gran dureza y son fáciles de limpiar, por lo que también se utilizan en encimeras, al igual que los materiales laminados y la madera tratada con barnices, aceites naturales o resinas. El mármol es otro material utilizado en la zona de trabajo de la cocina. Es resistente, aunque especialmente vulnerable a los ácidos y detergentes abrasivos. Otra piedra natural muy adecuada es el granito, puesto que no se mancha ni se raya y resulta inalterable en los cambios de temperatura. En la actualidad, existe una gran variedad de encimeras sintéticas, que reciben el nombre del fabricante, como el Ir'O, el Corian o el Silestone: materiales compuestos por minerales naturales y resinas que se adaptan a cualquier superficie. Las cocinas de nueva generación apuestan por materiales como el cristal securizado y el metacrilato. El suelo debe ser muy resistente a las manchas y muy fácil de limpiar. El gres es un material muy sufrido y fácil de mantener; el Silestone y los materiales sintéticos son resistentes y ofrecen gran variedad de colores y la madera y el mármol embellecen el entorno, aunque deben ser tratados con regularidad. El parquet sintético resulta también una buena opción.

THE OFFICE

Nowadays, the kitchen has become the place where the family gets together. The gradual decline of the dining room as the exclusive room for eating and getting together in, has granted greater prominence to the kitchen. In many modern homes, affording a dining area in the kitchen, the so-called office, for breakfast or other meals, is considered essential. There are practical solutions for situating the dining area in the kitchen, even though little space is available. In small, rectangular kitchens, a mobile bar for eating as well as for working, can be situated in front of the cooking area. Shelves for stowing away the breakfast items can be installed over it. In L-shaped kitchens, the office may be placed in one of the angles, and finished off with a bench that occupies the full length of the zone. It is a good option as it makes maximum use of the space and permits many diners at the same time. Situating the office on the work island is a very good choice, as is also, converting the work area or part of the counter, into one. Another solution for small kitchens is to place the office table up against the wall and surround it with cabinets. Yet another, is to place a small breakfast bar on top of the counter with small legs as supports. For kitchens with a minimum of space there are pull-out shelves which can become practical breakfast tables. Useful complements for the office are fold-up chairs without armrests or stools that take up little space, and can be concealed under the counter. In large kitchens with ample square meters, the ideal option is to sufficiently separate the office from the cooking zone in order to avoid grease and odors. Here, an independent space can be reserved but at the same time integrated into the kitchen. A minimum space of four square meters is needed so that four people can comfortably dine. A table with a rounded shape is the most practical since it takes maximum advantage of the space available in the corners. If the office is situated away from the cooking area, natural and more delicate materials such as wood and natural fibers, can be the choice for the furniture. This will grant more warmth and comfort to the ambience.

ESSBEREICH

Heutzutage ist die Küche der Ort, in welchem die Familie sich trifft. Das zunehmende Verschwinden des Esszimmers als ausschließlichem Ort für die Einnahme der Mahlzeiten und Familienversammlungen erhöht die Bedeutung der Küche. In vielen Küchen betrachtet man die Einrichtung eines Essbereichs für das Frühstück und andere Mahlzeiten als wesentlich. Es gibt sehr praktische Lösungen für das Integrieren eines Essbereichs, selbst dann, wenn nicht viel Platz zur Verfügung steht. In einem rechteckigen, wenn auch wenige Quadratmeter umfassendem Grundriss kann man eine verschiebbare Theke als Arbeits- und Essfläche vor den Kochbereich installieren. Darüber lassen sich Regale anbringen, in denen man alles für das Frühstück verstauen kann. In L-förmigen Küchen kann man den Essbereich in einer der Ecken unterbringen, indem man eine verschiebbare Bank längs der Ecke anbringt. Dies ist eine praktische Lösung, da der vorhandene Raum optimal genutzt wird und mehrere Gäste gleichzeitig Platz finden. Den Essbereich in einer Arbeitsinsel unterzubringen ist eine gute Möglichkeit, genauso wie das Verwandeln von Teilen des Arbeitsbereiches oder der Arbeitsplatte in einen kleinen Essbereich. Eine andere Lösung für kleine Küchen besteht darin, einen Tisch an der Wand anzubringen und mit einer Schrankstruktur zu umgeben oder auch im Installieren einer kleinen Frühstückstheke auf der Arbeitsplatte, die man durch Unterlagepunkte oder Querlatten anhebt. Für Kleinstküchen wurden herausnehmbare Platten erdacht, welche sich in praktische, kleine Frühstückstische verwandeln lassen. Nützliches Zubehör für diese kleinen Essbereiche sind zusammenklappbare Stühle ohne Armlehnen oder Hocker, die wenig Platz benötigen und sich unter der Theke verstecken lassen. Stehen mehr Quadratmeter für die Küche zur Verfügung ist es ratsam den Kochbereich vom Essbereich möglichst weit zu entfernen, um Fettspritzer und Gerüche von dort fernzuhalten, und so einen, obwohl noch in der Küche integrierten, dennoch unabhängigen Platz zu schaffen. Man braucht mindestens vier Quadratmeter Platz, um einen Tisch unterbringen zu können, an dem vier Personen bequem essen können. Am besten eignet sich ein Tisch mit abgerundeten Formen, da er für den Sitzenden am bequemsten ist. Wenn der Essbereich vom Arbeitsbereich getrennt ist, ist es möglich, etwas empfindlichere Möbel aus natürlichen Materialien wie Holz oder Naturfaser zu verwenden, da diese der Umgebung mehr Wärme und Komfort geben.

L'OFFICE

Aujourd'hui la cuisine est un lieu ou la famille se réuni. La disparition des salles à manger en tant que seul endroit où l'on prend ses repas lui donne un rôle plus important. Dans de nombreuses cuisines modernes on considère un coin à manger comme indispensable. Il y a des solutions très pratiques pour l'intégrer même si l'espace est restreint. Dans une petite cuisine rectangulaire, on peut placer un bar en face des fourneaux pouvant servir aussi bien pour manger que pour travailler. Des rayons installés au-dessus permettent de ranger ce dont on a besoin pour le petit déjeuner. Dans une cuisine en forme de L on peut placer le coin à manger dans l'un des angles en y mettant un banc permettant à plusieurs personnes de s'asseoir et d'utiliser l'endroit au maximum. Intégrer l'endroit où l'on mange dans l'îlot de travail est une bonne idée aussi bien que de convertire le plan de travail ou une partie du comptoir en un petit coin à manger. Une autre solution pour les petites cuisines, consiste à adosser une petite table à la paroi et à l'entourer d'armoires, ou de prolonger le comptoir par un petit bar avec des supports légers pour le petit déjeuner. Si l'espace est très réduit il existe des surfaces extractibles ou amovibles pouvant être converties en petites tables où l'on peut manger. Des chaises pliantes sans accoudoirs ou des tabourets prenant peu de place et pouvant être dissimulés sous le comptoir, s'avèrent êtres des accessoires très utiles. Pour les cuisines de grande dimension, il est conseillé d'éloigner le coin à manger des fourneaux, afin d'éviter les graisses et les odeurs en créant un espace indépendant qui est pourtant intégré à la cuisine. Un espace de 4 m^2 au minimus étant nécessaire à quatre personnes pour manger aisément. En choisissant une table ronde on peut tirer un avantage optimal dans les angles. Si le coin à manger est suffisamment éloigné delà zone où l'on travaille, on peut y placer des meubles réalisés avec des matériaux naturels et plus délicats en bois et fibres naturelles conférant à l'endroit plus de confort ainsi qu'une atmosphère plus chaleureuse.

EL OFFICE

La cocina constituye en la actualidad el lugar de reunión familiar. La desaparición progresiva del comedor como una habitación exclusiva para la comida y centro de reunión ha añadido mayor protagonismo a esta estancia. Muchas cocinas actuales consideran esencial organizar el comedor en la cocina u office para el desayuno y las otras comidas. Existen soluciones muy prácticas para ubicar esta zona comedor en la cocina, aún cuando no se dispone de mucho espacio. En cocinas de pocos metros que disponen de planta rectangular puede ubicarse una barra corrida delante de la zona de fuegos, de forma que pueda servir para comer y también como zona de trabajo. Sobre la barra pueden instalarse unas baldas donde puede almacenarse el servicio de desayuno. Para las cocinas en forma de L, el office puede situarse en uno de los ángulos, situando un banco corrido a lo largo del rincón. Resulta una buena opción puesto que se aprovecha al máximo el espacio y permite dar cabida a muchos comensales. Ubicar la zona office en la isla de trabajo es un buen recurso, igual que convertir el área de trabajo o parte de la encimera en pequeño comedor. Otra solución para cocinas con pocos metros consiste en adosar la mesa office a la pared y rodearla con una estructura de armarios, o bien colocar una pequeña barra de desayuno sobre la encimera de trabajo, elevándola con barrotes o puntos de apoyo. Para cocinas con el mínimo espacio se han creado baldas extraíbles que pueden convertirse en prácticas mesitas de desayuno. Los complementos útiles para el office son sillas plegables sin reposabrazos, o taburetes que ocupan poco sitio y pueden ocultarse debajo de la barra. En el caso de las cocinas que disponen de más metros, lo ideal es alejar el office de la zona de cocción para evitar las grasas y los olores, y así poder reservar un espacio independiente aunque integrado en la cocina. Se requiere de un espacio mínimo de 4 m^2 para situar una mesa donde puedan comer cómodamente cuatro comensales. Lo más práctico es utilizar una mesa de formas redondeadas: resultan más prácticas porque aprovechan los rincones. Si el office está separado de la zona de trabajo de la cocina, pueden elegirse muebles realizados con materiales naturales y un poco más delicados, como la madera y las fibras naturales, puesto que le añadirán más calidez y comodidad al ambiente.

KITCHEN ILLUMINATION

Just as in the bathroom, what is most pleasant is natural light, as it allows you to comfortably do the food preparation, especially at breakfast time or at midday. Therefore, if there are exterior windows, it is very advisable to take advantage of this source of natural light. To maintain privacy, curtains, lace curtains or curtains made of other thin fabrics, which allow the passage of light, can be installed. A kitchen requires various types of artificial light. Firstly, general overall lighting is needed in the room. Halogen spotlights are a good option since they afford a continuous light, which is very similar to natural. The work area or counter is in need of specific illumination as the food is cleaned and prepared here. Under the upper cabinets built-in, halogen spotlights or incandescent tubes can be installed. In the absence of upper cabinets, wall lights can be used or lamps with a shade hanging from the ceiling. The shade would have to be of a durable material. In order to be able to cook well, the cooking area must be well illuminated. Extractor hoods generally are equipped with halogen lights. Other sources of light can be installed, but they must be protected from splashing. If it is a large kitchen with a cooking island, hanging lamps can be used, or a hanging shelf, equipped with different light sources, can be installed. If you want to highlight the glass cabinets, halogen spotlights can be installed in the interior, as long as there is a cornice to hide the installation. Normally, the majority of these modules incorporate their own illumination. If the kitchen has an office area, it is important to choose soft lighting to afford a warm and cosy atmosphere. Excessively bright lightbulbs are not advisable as they give off too much heat and blind you. If the office is a small space, a table lamp approximately 70 or 80 cm over the table will suffice. If the area is large, there will be a need for extra lighting.

BELEUCHTUNG IN DER KÜCHE

Natürliches Licht ist in der Küche wie auch im Bad das angenehmste, da es – gerade zur Frühstücks- und zur Mittagszeit – für die Speisezubereitung am komfortabelsten ist. Wenn man über Fenster nach außen verfügt, ist es darum ratsam, diese natürliche Lichtquelle zu nutzen. Man kann, um die Ungestörtheit zu gewährleisten, Vorhänge und Gardinen aus feinem lichtdurchlässigem Stoff anbringen. Die Küche benötigt verschiedene Lichtquellen. Zum einen ist eine generelle Beleuchtung notwendig, um eine allgemeine Ausleuchtung zu erreichen. Halogenstrahler sind eine gute Wahl, da sie ein ständiges, der natürlichen Helligkeit sehr ähnliches Licht erzeugen. Die Arbeitsplatte bzw. der Arbeitsbereich benötigt allerdings eine punktuelle Beleuchtung, da dort das Essen vorbereitet wird. Man kann Halogenstrahler oder eine Leuchtstoffröhre in oder unter den Hängeschränken einbauen. Sollten keine Hängeschränke vorhanden sein, ist es möglich, eine Wandleuchte zu installieren oder eine Hängelampe an der Decke anzubringen, deren Schirm allerdings aus einem widerstandsfähigem Material sein sollte. Auch der Herd sollte während des Kochens beleuchtbar sein, damit der Garzustand der Lebensmittel genau begutachtet werden kann. Dunstabzugshauben sind daher normalerweise mit Halogenlampen ausgestattet. Eine andere Alternative ist das Anbringen eines Strahlers an einer vor Spritzern geschützten Stelle. Im Falle einer weiträumigen Küche mit zentraler Insel kann man diese mittels einer von der Decke hängenden Lampe beleuchten oder in ein über der Insel installiertes Hängeregal mehrere Strahler einbauen. Um Vitrinen hervorzuheben, kann man in ihrem Inneren Halogenstrahler installieren – sofern sie über ein Gesims verfügen, in welchem man die Kabel verstecken kann. Normalerweise sind in der Mehrheit der heute angebotenen Module bereits Beleuchtungselemente eingebaut. Sollte die Küche einen Essbereich besitzen, ist es wichtig, diesen mit einer weichen Beleuchtung auszustatten, um so eine warme und gemütliche Atmosphäre zu schaffen. Die Verwendung von zu starken Glühbirnen ist nicht ratsam, da diese sehr viel Hitze abstrahlen und blenden können. Wenn der Essbereich nicht viel Platz einnimmt, reicht es, eine Lampe ca. 70 bis 80 cm über dem Tisch aufzuhängen. Sollte der Essbereich größer sein wäre eine zusätzliche Beleuchtung notwendig.

L'ÉCLAIRAGE DANS LA CUISINE

Tout comme dans la salle de bains, la lumière naturelle est la plus agréable. Elle permet de préparer les repas, en particulier le matin et à midi, de façon plaisante. Lorsqu'on dispose de fenêtres donnant sur l'extérieur, il est conseillé de jouir des avantages de cette source d'éclairage. On peut préserver une certaine intimité en mettant des rideaux légers permettant le passage de la lumière. Une cuisine requière divers types de lumières. Pour commencer, un éclairage général illuminant toute la pièce. Des spots halogènes procurent une luminosité constante, très semblable à la lumière du jour. Pour le comptoir ou le plan de travail on a besoin d'un éclairage ponctuel nécessaire à la préparation et au nettoyage des aliments. On peut intégrer des spots sous les armoires suspendues, ou y fixer des tubes néon. En absence d'armoires supérieures, on peut installer un abat-jour au plafond ou une applique contre le mur. Les fourneaux et la cuisinière doivent également être éclairés permettant de contrôler la cuisson des mets. Les hottes de ventilation étant en général équipées de lampes halogènes. On peut y installer d'autres points de lumière en les protégeant contre les éclaboussures. Dans une cuisine ample avec un îlot central, on peut illuminer celui-ci au moyen d'une lampe fixée au plafond ou de spots intégrés dans une étagère suspendue au-dessus de cet élément. Pour mettre en évidence les vitrines dans les armoires supérieures, on peut y placer des spots à l'intérieurs si l'on dispose d'un canal permettant de cacher l'installation. Normalement la majorité des modules ont leur propre éclairage. Si la cuisine dispose d'un coin à manger, il est important de choisir une lumière douce pour créer une atmosphère chaude et agréable. L'emploi d'ampoules trop puissantes est déconseillé. Elles éblouissent et dégagent beaucoup de chaleur. Si l'endroit où l'on mange ne prend pas beaucoup de place, il suffit de placer une lampe à une distance de 70–80 cm au dessus de la table. Si l'espace est plus grand un éclairage supplémentaire est nécessaire.

LA ILUMINACIÓN EN LA COCINA

Al igual que en el cuarto de baño, la luz natural es la más agradecida en la cocina, puesto que permite preparar los alimentos con comodidad, especialmente durante el desayuno y al mediodía. Por ello, si se dispone de ventanas al exterior es muy aconsejable aprovechar esta fuente de luz natural, por lo que puede reservarse la intimidad utilizando cortinas y visillos con telas muy finas para que no impidan el paso de la luz. La cocina requiere de diversos tipos de luz artificial. Para empezar, la luz general es necesaria para iluminar globalmente la estancia. Los focos halógenos resultan una buena opción: proporcionan una luz continua muy parecida a la natural. La zona de trabajo o encimera requiere de una iluminación puntual, ya que es en ella donde se limpian y preparan los alimentos. Pueden colocarse focos halógenos empotrados bajo los armarios superiores, o bien situar en la zona tubos de luz incandescente. Si no se dispone de armarios superiores, puede colgarse una pantalla de techo, aunque debe ser de un material resistente, o bien puede colocarse un aplique. La zona de cocción debe estar iluminada mientras se cocina para comprobar el estado de los alimentos. Las campanas extractoras suelen estar equipadas con luces halógenas. Otra opción consiste en colocar otro punto de luz resguardado de las salpicaduras. En el caso de disponer de una cocina amplia con una isla en el centro, ésta puede iluminarse mediante lámparas colgantes o un estante suspendido sobre la isla, en el que pueden colocarse varios puntos de luz. Para realzar las vitrinas en los armarios superiores, pueden colocarse focos halógenos en su interior, siempre y cuando se disponga de una cornisa para ocultar la instalación. Por norma general, la mayoría de módulos ya incorporan su propia iluminación. Si la cocina tiene una zona office, es importante elegir un tipo de iluminación suave para recrear un ambiente cálido y acogedor. No son aconsejables bombillas demasiado potentes porque dan mucho calor y pueden deslumbrar. Si el office no ocupa mucho espacio, bastará con colocar una lámpara sobre la mesa, que debe quedar a unos 70 u 80 cm por encima de la mesa. Si la superficie es más grande, se necesitarán lámparas de apoyo.

KITCHEN
AND A

Appareils
électro-ménagers
et accessoires
de cuisine

Elektrogeräte und
Zubehörteile in der Küche

APPLIANCES
CESSORIES

*Electrodomésticos
y complementos
de la cocina*

KITCHEN STOVES AND ESTRACTOR HOODS

As with all appliances, the kitchen stove should be chosen bearing in mind the needs of the users. This multi-use device for cooking food is available with gas burners or electric hotplates or a combination of both. In some of the newer models, easy-to-clean, gas burners have reappeared with a modern design. Many models even allow the burners and the grates to be cleaned in the dishwasher. Whether gas or electric, the latest stoves also include numerous accessories or cooking modules such as an oven, a fryer, a grill, a grate and systems for steam cooking which eliminate the need for skillets and saucepans. All in all, they allow the food to be cooked in a very natural way. Accessories such as hotplates for keeping prepared dishes hot are also available. Glass-ceramic ranges are the modern version of burners and they feature rapid cooking and innovative design. Extractor hoods are indispensable for the cooking zone. Nowadays, they are quiet and powerful. There is a very complete range of models available, which even include compact, fold-away and extra-flat models. Normally they are made of stainless steel and usually come with halogen spotlights built-in for illuminating the cooking area. Recently, small extractors have appeared, which are mounted on a telescopic, swivel arm and allow you to extract fumes from the precise origen.

HERDE, ÖFEN UND DUNSTABZUGSHAUBEN

Wie alle Elektrogeräte sollte man auch den Herd nach den Bedürfnissen der Benutzer auswählen. Dieser vielfältig verwendbare Apparat zur Zubereitung der Speisen hat elektrische oder mit Gas betriebene Kochplatten oder bietet eine Kombination aus beiden Systemen. Die neuesten Entwürfe haben die Gasherde wiederentdeckt, und erlauben ein attraktives Design bei einfacher Reinigung: Ofenrost und Brenner vieler Modelle lassen sich im Geschirrspüler säubern. Ob mit Gas oder elektrisch betrieben, für die Herde werden heute eine Vielzahl Zubehörteile und Kochmodule angeboten, wie vor allem der Ofen, aber auch Dampfkochsysteme, Friteusen, Bleche sowie Grill- und Ofenroste, mit denen die Lebensmittel ohne Töpfe und Pfannen und so auf sehr natürliche Weise zubereitet werden können, oder den Tellerwärmer zum Warmhalten der zubereiteten Speisen. Das Ceranfeld ist die moderne Version der ursprünglichen Herde und zeichnet sich durch Beschleunigung des Kochvorgangs und neuartiges Design aus. Absolut unabdingbar im Kochbereich ist die Dunstabzugshaube. Sie ist leise und sehr leistungsstark; es gibt sehr große Modelle, aber auch kompakt gehaltene, extraflache und sogar klappbare. Normalerweise werden sie aus rostfreiem Stahl hergestellt und so gut wie alle Modelle haben eingebaute Halogenstrahler zur Beleuchtung des Kochbereichs. Unter den letzten Neuheiten findet man Dunstabzüge mit einem teleskopischen, drehbaren Arm, der das Absaugen der Dämpfe und Gerüche direkt am Entstehungsort erlaubt.

CUISINIÈRES ET HOTTES DE VENTILATION

Comme avec tous les appareils électro-ménagers on doit choisir la cuisinière en fonction des besoins de l'utilisateur. Cet appareil à usages multiples permettant la préparation des mets, comprend des plaques chauffantes électrique ou à gaz, ou une combinaison des deux systèmes. On a redécouvert l'utilisation du gaz pour les nouveaux modèles de cuisinières. Elles s'adaptent aux dernières tendances, ont des lignes attrayantes permettant pourtant un nettoyage facile. Les brûleurs et les grilles de nombreux modèles peuvent être nettoyés dans le lave-vaisselle. Qu'elle soit à gaz ou électrique, la cuisinière a un grand nombre d'accessoires et d'options de cuisson en commençant par le four, les systèmes de cuisson à la vapeur et en passant par la friteuse et le gril qui permettent la préparation des aliments sans avoir à employer de casseroles ou de poêle et de les cuire de façon naturelle. Il y a également comme accessoires, des chauffe-plats permettant de réchauffer et de garder les assiettes au chaud. Les plaques vitro-ceran sont l'une des versions les plus modernes dans le domaine des plaques chauffantes et se différentie par une cuisson rapide et un design inédit. La hotte de ventilation est un appareil indispensable dans la cuisine. Elle est peu bruyante et très puissante. Il en existe de très grandes, de plus compactes, des extra-minces de même que des modèles télescopiques. Elles sont en général en acier inoxydable et ont des spots halogènes intégrés qui éclairent la cuisinière. Parmi les dernières nouveautés il existe des modèles à bras télescopique et pivotant permettant de capter les odeurs et les vapeurs à la source.

COCINAS, HORNOS Y CAMPANAS EXTRACTORAS

Como todos los electrodomésticos, la cocina debe elegirse en función del uso que va a hacerse de ella. Este aparato multiuso, dedicado a la cocción de alimentos, puede tener hornillos eléctricos o placas de gas, o bien una combinación de ambos sistemas. Los nuevos diseños de placas de cocción han recuperado los fogones a gas con líneas atractivas que permiten una limpieza fácil: muchos modelos permiten que los quemadores y las parrillas puedan introducirse en el lavavajillas. Sean de gas o eléctricas, las placas incorporan un buen número de accesorios o módulos de cocción como el propio horno, freidoras, planchas, parrillas y sistemas de cocción al vapor que permiten preparar los alimentos sin usar ningún tipo de sartén o cacerola y consiguen un alimento cocinado muy natural. También hay accesorios como el calientaplatos, que se utiliza para mantener calientes los platos recién cocinados. La vitrocerámica es la versión moderna de la cocina con fogones, y se diferencia de ella por su rápida cocción y su novedoso diseño. Un accesorio totalmente imprescindible para la zona de fuegos es la campana extractora. Silenciosas y muy potentes, existen modelos muy amplios o compactos, abatibles o extraplanos. Se fabrican generalmente en acero inoxidable y casi todos los modelos disponen de focos halógenos empotrados para iluminar la zona de cocción. Entre las novedades, existen pequeños modelos de extractor equipados con un brazo giratorio telescópico que permite aspirar humos y vapores en el mismo lugar donde se producen.

REFRIGERATORS AND DISHWASHERS

The latest refrigerators come in various sizes, from 85 cm high to 2 m in the case of the so-called combis, refrigerators with two separate, independent motors, one for the refrigerator and one for the freezer. The capacity varies depending on the model and the range. Some of the most innovative models incorporate what is called no-frost, which is a dry air, refrigeration system that avoids the need for defrosting. Other novelties are electronic systems for regulating the interior temperature. Some companies are bringing out "intelligent" refrigerators equipped with a computer and touch screen on the door, which allows you to check the status and even control the expiration date of the food. The fridges that make use of interactive technology can be connected to Internet, some include radio and television, and others permit you to activate and program the device by telephone. In the so-called side by side models, the different compartments are kept at distinct temperatures, and the outside door incorporates an ice cube dispenser and a cold water font. In some of the latest models we can find diverse and unusual colors, stainless steel or metalic finishes and even some touches of glass in the finish, and features such as transparent freezer drawers, so that the contents are always easily visible. Dishwashers are also undergoing much innovation. They are available now with greater capacity, variable temperature ranges and more than ten different washing programs. Advances afford cleaner dishes and shinier glasses without stains. There are fast programs and electronic systems, which calculate optimum water and electricity consumption. The latest designs also include models with the exterior encasement made entirely of stainless steel.

KÜHLSCHRÄNKE UND GESCHIRRSPÜLER

Die neuen Kühlschränke haben sehr unterschiedliche Größen (von 85 cm Höhe bis zu 2 m Höhe im Falle der Kühl- und Gefrierkombinationen mit je einem unabhängigen Motor für das Gefrierfach und den Kühlschrank). Die Kapazität unterscheidet sich je nach Modell, genauso wie die angebotenen Einzelfunktionen. Die neuesten Modelle sind mit No-Frost ausgestattet, einem Kühlungssystem mittels kalter trockener Luft, wodurch der Kühlschrank nicht mehr abgetaut werden muss. Eine andere Neuerung sind elektronische Systeme, welche die Innentemperatur regulieren. Einige Firmen bieten „intelligente" Kühlschränke mit einem Computer und einem Touch-Screen in der Kühlschranktür an, um die automatische Kontrolle der eingelagerten Lebensmittel zu ermöglichen. Diese mit interaktiver Technologie ausgestatteten Kühlschränke können mit dem Internet verbunden werden, einige Modelle haben Radio und Fernseher mit an Bord und andere lassen sich per Telefon bedienen und programmieren. Die sogenannten side by side Modelle bieten Fächer mit unterschiedlichen Temperaturen und frontal eingebaute Eiswürfel- und Kaltwasserspender an. Was das Design betrifft, gibt es spektakuläre Neuerungen. Die neuesten Modelle werden in Ausfertigungen aus rostfreiem Stahl, in Metallic oder verschiedenen Farben vertrieben, mit Glasdetails oder durchsichtigen Gefrierfächern, die das darin Aufbewahrte sichtbar lassen. Auch die Geschirrspüler haben Neues zu bieten: größere Kapazität, verschiedene Spültemperaturen und mehr als 10 unterschiedliche Spülprogramme. Sie sind mit einer Technik ausgestattet, die Teller und Gläser fleckenlos brillieren lässt, mit Schnellspülprogrammen und Elektronik, welche die optimale Wasser- und Strommenge errechnet. Die innovativsten Modelle haben ein Gehäuse, das komplett aus rostfreiem Stahl besteht.

RÉFRIGÉRATEURS ET LAVE-VAISSELLES

Les nouveaux réfrigérateurs sont de tailles très différentes (ils vont de 85 cm à 2 m de haut pour des appareils combinés frigo-congélateurs ayant deux moteurs indépendants). La capacité diffère d'un modèle à l'autre de même que la puissance. Les nouveaux appareils sont pourvus d'un système rendant le dégivrage superflu grâce à un mode de refroidissement au moyen d'air froid et sec. Une autre innovation est l'apparition de systèmes électroniques qui règlent automatiquement la température intérieure. Certaines maisons proposent des réfrigérateurs « intelligents » qui à l'aide d'un écran et de touches intégrées à la porte permettent un control automatique et indique la date d'expiration des denrées emmagasinées. Certains ayant une technologie interactive peuvent même être branchés sur l'internet et d'autre sont pourvu de radio, de télévision où se laissent activer ou programmer par téléphone. Les modèles dit « side by side » ont des compartiments à températures différentes et un distributeur d'eau ou de cube de glace intégrée sur l'avant. Concernant le design il existe des innovations spectaculaires. Les dernières en date proposent des exemplaires en acier inoxydable de couleur métallique ou d'autres, avec des détailles et des accessoires en verre, ainsi que des compartiments transparents laissant voir ce qui est entreposé. Les lave-vaisselles également offrent des nouveautés. Une capacité plus grande, différentes températures de lavages et une dizaine de programmes à choix. Ils sont équipés de systèmes permettant de nettoyer et faire briller les verres et les assiettes, de programmes rapides et de systèmes électroniques permettant de calculer de façon optimale le débit d'eau et d'électricité. Les derniers modèles sont entièrement en acier inoxydable.

FRIGORÍFICOS Y LAVAVAJILLAS

Los nuevos frigoríficos presentan medidas muy variadas (desde 85 cm de altura hasta combis –aparatos con los motores del refrigerador y el congelador independientes– de 2 metros). La capacidad varía en función de cada modelo, así como las prestaciones que ofrece. Los modelos más innovadores incorporan la función no-frost, un sistema de refrigeración por aire frío seco gracias al cual no se necesita descongelar el aparato. Otra novedad que ofrecen los modelos actuales es la incorporación de sistemas electrónicos que regulan la temperatura interior. Algunas firmas presentan neveras "inteligentes", equipadas con un ordenador y una pantalla táctil que, instalados en la puerta del aparato, permiten comprobar el estado e incluso controlar la caducidad de los alimentos. Estos frigoríficos que incorporan tecnología interactiva pueden conectarse a Internet, algunos modelos incorporan radio y televisión, y otros permiten activar y programar el aparato a través del teléfono. Los llamados "side by side" ofrecen compartimentos con temperaturas distintas y dispensadores frontales de cubitos y agua fresca. En cuanto al diseño, presentan espectaculares innovaciones. Los más actuales se comercializan con acabados en acero inoxidable, metalizados o de distintos colores, con detalles de cristal, o congeladores con cajones transparentes para visualizar lo que se guarda en el interior… Los lavavajillas también presentan novedades: mayor capacidad, varias temperaturas y más de 10 programas de lavado, y están equipados con sistemas que dejan platos y vasos brillantes y sin manchas, con lavado rápido y un sistema electrónico que calcula la cantidad óptima de agua y electricidad. Los más innovadores disponen de una carcasa realizada íntegramente en acero inoxidable.

SINKS AND FIXTURES

When choosing a kitchen sink, the following should be taken into consideration: the amount of space available, the number of basins required, and the type of material which will best fit in with the general design of the kitchen. Nowadays, numerous models are available, ranging from small sinks, which occupy little space, to very large ones. Some makes afford the possibility of a customized size, whereas others incorporate the colander into the sink design. Some designs provide a large sink, and a smaller one for cleaning vegetables. Still others incorporate a cullender and also a tray, which can be placed over the basin when not in use, so as to provide an extra work surface. Yet others have small sinks and inserts for leftover food. Sinks installed in a right angle of the kitchen counter, so-called corner sinks, afford maximum use of available space, which is an ideal option when the dimensions of the room are small. Some offer a sink and counter which is all one solid piece, thus eliminating any joints between the two. Nowadays many designs are made of steel, although stoneware and synthetic materials are also employed. In regards to kitchen fixtures, there is a wide variety of models and diverse features on offer: long-stem, rotating, pull-out, mixer taps, or the traditional dual tap. A long stem tap is very practical and pull-out taps greatly facilitate kitchen tasks. We can opt for a matt, chrome, gold-like, or white lacquer finish. The design itself may be very contemporary, or colonial, classical, or daringly minimalist.

ARMATUREN UND SPÜLEN

Maßgeblich für die Wahl der Spüle sind der verfügbare Platz, die Anzahl der erforderlichen Becken sowie das Material, das zum Stil der Küche passen sollte. Der Markt bietet eine Vielzahl von Modellen, die sehr wenig Platz einnehmen, oder auch große Spülen. Bei einigen Herstellern kann man sie nach Maß anfertigen lassen, bei anderen verschmelzen in einer Einheit Spülbecken und Abtropffläche. Einige hervorragend ausgestattete Designs sehen ein großes Becken, ein kleineres zum Gemüsewaschen, eine Abtropffläche sowie eine praktische Abdeckplatte vor, mit der die Spüle bei Nichtbenutzung abgedeckt werden kann, um die Arbeitsfläche zu vergrößern. Andere Modelle haben kleine Becken und einen Einsatz für Essensreste. Sehr praktisch sind in der Ecke angebrachte Spülen, denn so kann der Raum zwischen den Arbeitsflächen genutzt werden. Diese Modelle sind eine gute Wahl in kleinen Küchen. Einige Hersteller bieten fugenlose Spülen und Arbeitsflächen an, die aus einem Stück bestehen. Zahlreiche Modelle werden aus Stahl hergestellt, aber auch Steinzeug und Kunststoff sind erhältlich. Küchenarmaturen kann man ebenfalls aus einer breiten Produktpalette mit unterschiedlichen Funktionen auswählen: Armaturen mit langem, schwenkbarem oder ausziehbarem Auslauf, Einhand- oder Dreilochbatterie. Modelle mit hohem Auslauf sind im Küchengebrauch sehr praktisch, und ausziehbare Brausen sind äußerst bequem in der Handhabung. Armaturen gibt es in verschiedenen Ausführungen: matt, verchromt, mit Vergoldungen, weiß lackiert. Das Design der Küchenarmaturen kann den aktuellen Trends folgen, es gibt sie im Kolonialstil, mit klassischen Formen oder in gewagten minimalistischen Designs.

119

EVIERS ET ROBINETS

Pour choisir l'évier on doit tenir compte de l'espace disponible, du nombre de plonges désirées et du matériel qui ira le mieux avec le style général de la cuisine. Sur le marché, on trouve une infinité de modèles, de petite ou de grande taille occupant plus ou moins de place. Certaines marques permettent de commander un évier sur mesure, d'autres proposent des éviers et égouttoirs d'une pièce ; quelques-uns sont très bien équipés et disposent d'une grande plonge, d'une plus petite pour nettoyer les légumes, d'un égouttoir et d'une planche pouvant être placée au dessus de l'évier, permettant lorsqu'il n'est pas employé d'agrandir le plan de travail. Certains modèles ont de petits bacs avec couvercles incorporés pour les déchets. Les éviers d'angle s'avèrent être très pratiques permettant d'utiliser un coin entre les plans de travail. Ces modèles nommés également éviers de coins sont une bonne solution pour les petites cuisines. Certaines maisons réalisent des éviers et plans de travail d'une pièce. Beaucoup d'entre eux sont en acier bien qu'il en existe aussi en grès ou en matériaux synthétiques. Pour la robinetterie de cuisine on dispose également d'une grande variété de modèles d'utilité diverse : des robinets à bras longs, giratoires, extractibles mitigeurs et mélangeurs. Ceux à bras longs sont très pratiques dans la cuisine de même qu'un modèle extractible permet un travail aisé. Ils ont une finition mate, chromée, dorée ou en vernis blanc. Suivant le design, la robinetterie peut être très moderne, de style colonial, de forme classique ou audacieuse et minimaliste.

GRIFERÍAS Y FREGADEROS

Para elegir el fregadero debe tenerse en cuenta el espacio del que se dispone, cuántas cubetas se necesitan y el material que combinará mejor con el estilo general de la cocina. En el mercado puede encontrarse infinidad de modelos que ocupan muy poco espacio y fregaderos de gran tamaño. Algunas marcas permiten encargar un fregadero a medida, otras incorporan en una misma pieza fregadero y escurridor; algunos diseños muy bien equipados se dividen en una cubeta grande, otra más pequeña para limpiar verduras, un escurridor y una práctica bandeja, que puede colocarse encima del fregadero, cuando éste no se utiliza, para aumentar la superficie de trabajo. Otros modelos incorporan pequeñas cubetas con tapa para los restos de comida. Los fregaderos instalados en ángulo resultan muy prácticos, puesto que permiten aprovechar un rincón de la encimera. Estos modelos, llamados también fregaderos esquineros, son una buena elección si la cocina dispone de pocos metros. Algunas firmas realizan fregaderos y encimeras sin juntas, de una sola pieza. Muchos diseños se fabrican en acero, aunque también los hay de gres y de materiales sintéticos. Las griferías de cocina también disponen de una variada oferta de modelos de diversas prestaciones: griferías de caño largo, giratorio, extraíble, monomandos, bimandos... Los diseños de caños muy altos son muy prácticos en la cocina, aunque un modelo extraíble permite trabajar con gran comodidad. Las hay de acabado mate, cromado, con toques dorados, lacados en blanco... En cuanto a su diseño, las griferías de cocina pueden ser de estéticas muy actuales, de estilo colonial, de formas clásicas o de atrevidos diseños minimalistas.

SMALL ELECTRIC APPLIANCES

Conventional ovens have a heating element at the top and at the bottom of the oven which heats the food. Microwave ovens, on the other hand, irradiate heat over the food, which cooks and browns the food at the same time. In a microwave oven, the heating comes directly from the food, so the food does not have the same browned appearance as it does with a conventional oven. Cooking is very fast in a microwave and so the electricity consumption is reduced. The simplest models heat, thaw and cook whereas other models incorporate a grill for browning, energy saving systems, an ultra-fast thaw setting and programs for specific foods. They may even include specific accessories such as trays, grates and others, to facilitate cooking. There are models, which are a combination microwave-traditional oven all in one, which is ideal for small kitchens. Innovation is also present in small appliances, which make the work area more practical. There are kitchen robots, beaters, grills and other useful electric devices, with silent, ever more powerful motors with variable velocities. Nowadays, there are innumerable small appliances available, such as completely safe sausage cutters which can be disassembled, fast kettles with an automatic switch-off, coffee-makers with a hotplate for heating up the cup or barbecues with easy-to-clean, non-sticking, pull-out grates.

KLEINE HAUSHALTSGERÄTE

Konventionelle Öfen garen die Lebensmittel mittels der oben und unten angebrachten Heizstäbe. Im Gegensatz dazu bestrahlen Mikrowellen die Lebensmittel mit Hitzestrahlen und bräunen und braten sie so gleichzeitig. Im Mikrowellenherd entsteht die Erhitzung direkt im Lebensmittel, so dass keine Bräunung wie im traditionellen Ofen erreicht wird. Kochen im Mikrowellenherd geht sehr schnell, der Stromverbrauch ist geringer. Einfache Geräte erhitzen, garen und tauen Gefrorenes auf; andere haben zusätzlich einen Grill zum Überbacken, Systeme für Stromersparnis, Programme für schnelles Auftauen oder spezielle Lebensmittel und sogar Utensilien, die das Kochen erleichtern, wie Grill- und Ofenroste oder Tabletts. Einige Modelle vereinen – ideal für kleine Küchen – Mikrowelle und traditionelles Kochen in einem Gerät. Neuheiten in der Küche erstrecken sich auch auf Elektrogeräte, welche den Arbeitsbereich praktischer gestalten. Küchenroboter, Mixer, Grillplatten und andere Geräte haben vielfältige Funktionen und bereichern den Arbeitsplatz durch stärkere und leisere Motoren sowie verschiedene Geschwindigkeitsstufen. Das Angebot an Kleinstgeräten geht ins Unendliche. Es gibt auseinandernehmbare Wurst- und Brotschneidemaschinen mit Vorrichtungen, die ihren Gebrauch absolut sicher machen, immer schnellere Wasserkocher mit Abschaltautomatik, Kaffeemaschinen mit Tassenwarmhalteplatten oder Grillöfen mit zur einfacheren Reinigung herausnehmbaren antihaftbeschichteten Platten.

PETITS APPAREILS ÉLECTRO-MÉNAGERS

Les fours conventionnels cuisent les aliments au moyen de corps chauffants placés dans les parties supérieure et inférieure de l'appareil. Les fours micro-ondes au contraire projettent des ondes sur les aliments les cuisant et les dorant en même temps. La cuisson de l'aliment est directe et ne présente pas le même aspect doré que dans un four traditionnel. Elle est très rapide et la consommation électrique est très réduite. Les appareils plus simples réchauffent, dégèlent et cuisent, d'autres modèles ont un gril incorporé pour gratiner, des systèmes permettant d'économiser de l'énergie, de décongèlation ultra rapide, des programmes adaptés aux différents aliments … ainsi que des ustensiles facilitant leur cuisson : tels que plats, grilles etc. … Il existe des appareils combinant fours traditionnels et micro-onde idéals pour les petites cuisines. Il y a également des innovations dans les petits électro-ménagers qui simplifient le travail. Robots de cuisine, batteurs, barbecues, pour n'en citer que quelques-uns. Ils sont à vitesse réglable, ont des moteurs toujours plus puissants et sont de plus en plus silencieux. On trouve une infinité de petits électro-ménagers sur le marché allant de machines à couper le pain ou la charcuterie qui ont des dispositifs permettant de les utiliser en toute sécurité, des chauffe-eaux toujours plus rapides et qui se déclenchent automatiquement, des machines à café avec plaque chauffante pour les tasses, des barbecues avec des grilles amovibles et anti-adhésives faciles à nettoyer.

PEQUEÑOS ELECTRODOMÉSTICOS

Los hornos convencionales calientan el alimento a través de las planchas superiores e inferiores del aparato. A diferencia de éstos, los microondas irradian calor sobre el alimento y lo cuecen y doran al mismo tiempo. En el microondas, el calentamiento procede directamente del alimento, por lo que no presenta el mismo aspecto dorado del horno tradicional. La cocción en el microondas es muy rápida, por lo que el consumo es reducido. Los aparatos más sencillos calientan, descongelan y cocinan, aunque los otros modelos incorporan grill para gratinar, sistemas de ahorro de energía, descongelación ultrarrápida, programación según el alimento… e incluso añaden utensilios que facilitan su cocción: bandejas, guías, parrillas… Hay modelos que incorporan la cocción por microondas y horno tradicional en un mismo aparato, ideales para cocinas con pocos metros. La innovación distingue también los pequeños electrodomésticos, que convierten en más práctica la zona de trabajo. Robots de cocina, batidoras, planchas, teteras y demás útiles eléctricos presentan multitud de prestaciones, con diversos niveles de velocidad y potentes motores cada vez más silenciosos. El mercado ofrece un sinfín de pequeños electrodomésticos, como un cortafiambres desmontable con dispositivos que permiten utilizarlo con total seguridad, hervidores de agua de mayor rapidez y desconector automático, cafeteras con placas calienta-tazas o barbacoas con placas antiadherentes extraíbles para facilitar su limpieza.

KITCHEN ACCESSORIES

Nowadays, innumerable complementary items are available in order to make preparing and cooking in the kitchen easier. What is best is to always have at hand the tools and equipment needed. To this end, there are innumerable solutions: bars, rails and guides for hanging skimmers and kitchen towels from, shelves for the placement of jars for pasta and legumes, spice trays, etc. All type of accessories are available so that the kitchen can be kept neat and tidy. There are bottle racks, mini-cupboards for coffee services, small cabinets covered with a metalic sheet, and different modules on wheels for storing food in, or for carrying cooked dishes to the table on. Serving and auxiliary trolleys are very practical and offer a wide variety of designs. Some can be turned into a small counter for working on, and others have drawers and a high storage capacity. There are others that fold up in order to maximize space, others that have no back panel, and some that incorporate shelves, wings or pull-out trays. They are commonly made of steel or aluminum, even so, there are also designs made from wood and natural fibers. The choice of each accessory and auxiliary furniture module depends on the general style of the kitchen. There are some models for classifying and storing trash, and even for stowing away large items like saucepans and skillets. Stools are essential, above all, if the kitchen has an office zone. There is a wide variety available: stack-up, fold-up, anatomical, etc.

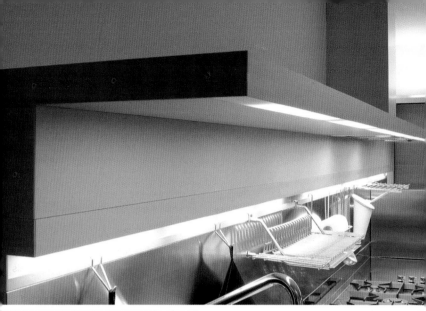

133

KÜCHENZUBEHÖR

Eine Fülle von Zubehörteilen vereinfacht das Vorbereiten und Kochen der Lebensmittel erheblich. Am praktischsten ist es, diese Instrumente und Werkzeuge immer griffbereit zu haben. Dafür gibt es eine Vielzahl von Lösungen: Stangen und Schienen zum Aufhängen von Schaumlöffeln und Lappen, Böden zur Aufbewahrung von Gefäßen mit Nudeln oder Hülsenfrüchten, Gewürzständer etc. Die Hersteller bieten alles erdenkliche Zubehör an, das hilft in der Küche immer Ordnung zu halten: Flaschenregale, Minischränke für das Kaffeeservice, kleine Schränke mit Drahtgeflecht und verschiedene Module auf Rädern, welche leicht zu bewegen sind und der Aufbewahrung von Lebensmitteln dienen oder das Servieren der frisch gekochten Speisen direkt am Tisch möglich machen. Diese Wägelchen sind sehr praktisch und in vielfältigen Designs zu haben: Einige bieten verschiedene Nutzungsmöglichkeiten mit kleinen Arbeitsplatten zum Schneiden der Lebensmittel, Schubladen und eine große Lagerkapazität; andere sind aus Gründen der Platzersparnis zusammenklappbar, haben Fächer, keine Rückwand, ausklappbare Flügel oder herausnehmbare Tabletts. Sie werden normalerweise aus Stahl oder Aluminium hergestellt, es gibt aber auch Modelle aus Holz oder Naturfaser. Die Auswahl des Zubehörs hängt vom Gesamtstil der Küche ab. Einige Modelle wurden zur Abfalltrennung entworfen, andere für die Aufbewahrung der größeren Utensilien, wie Pfannen und Töpfe. Hocker oder Sitzgelegenheiten sind – besonders in Küchen mit Essecke – unabdingbar; es gibt sie aufeinanderstellbar, zusammenklappbar, körpergerecht.

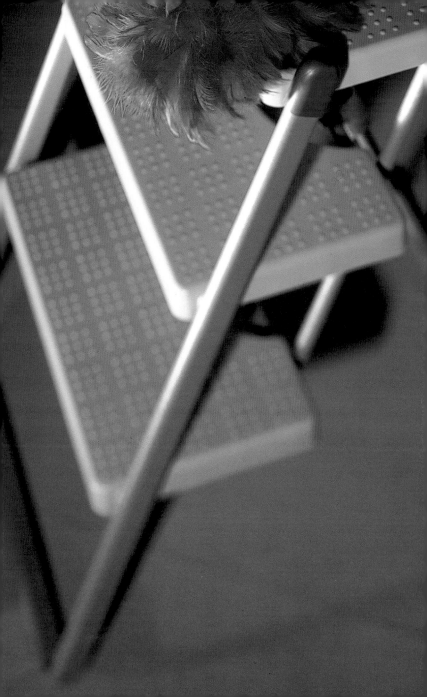

ACCESSOIRES DE CUISINE

Il existe une grande quantité d'accessoires et d'instruments simplifiant la préparation et la cuisson des aliments. Il est utile de les avoir à portée de main. De ce fait il y a plusieurs solutions : des barres et des rails auxquels on peut suspendre des louches ou des linges de cuisine, des rayons sur lesquels on peut ranger des boîtes de contenance diverse, des épices etc. ... Certaines maisons offrent une infinité d'accessoires permettant de maintenir la cuisine en ordre. Des petites armoires porte bouteilles, d'autres où l'on peut ranger les services de thé ou de café, certaines avec de portes métalliques, et également des modules sur roues, faciles à déplacer, permettant de ranger des denrées ou de servir à table les mets fraîchement préparés. Ces petits chariots sont très pratiques et on peut les obtenir dans une grande variété de design. Certains sont convertibles, avec de petits plans de travail permettant par exemple de couper des aliments, d'autres ont des tiroirs pouvant renfermer d'innombrables choses. Certains d'entre eux sont pliables avec casiers, sans parois arrière, avec des rayons amovibles pour en augmenter la capacité et permettant de les ranger facilement. Ces modules d'appoint sont généralement en acier ou en aluminium. Il en existe pourtant en bois ou en d'autres matériaux naturels. Le choix des accessoires dépend du style de la cuisine. Certains modèles permettent le trier les ordures, d'autres de ranger de grands ustensiles tels que casseroles et poêles. Des tabourets sont indispensables si on a un coin à manger. Il y a des modèles empilables, pliables, de forme anatomique.

ACCESORIOS DE COCINA

Existen múltiples complementos que hacen mucho más fácil preparar y cocinar los alimentos en la cocina. Lo más útil es tener siempre a mano los instrumentos y enseres de trabajo. Para ello existen multitud de soluciones: barras y rieles para colgar espumaderas y trapos de cocina, baldas para colocar botes de pasta y legumbres, especieros… Las firmas incorporan todo tipo de accesorios para que la cocina se mantenga siempre en orden: casilleros para guardar botellas, minialacenas para el juego de café, pequeños armarios con tela metálica y distintos módulos con ruedas, fácilmente transportables para guardar alimentos o servir los platos cocinados directamente a la mesa. Los carritos auxiliares son muy prácticos y ofrecen diseños muy variados: algunos son convertibles, con una pequeña encimera para cortar los alimentos, con cajones y gran capacidad de almacenamiento. Otros son plegables, para aprovechar al máximo el espacio, con baldas, sin trasera, con alas o bandejas extraíbles. Suelen realizarse en acero o aluminio, aunque también hay diseños en madera y fibras naturales. La elección de cada accesorio o mueble auxiliar depende del estilo general de la cocina. Algunos modelos se han fabricado con la intención de clasificar los residuos o incluso para almacenar los enseres más grandes, como cacerolas y paellas. Los taburetes son indispensables, en especial si la cocina tiene una zona office. Existen modelos apilables, plegables, anatómicos…

Pro
Projekte
PRO
Proye

Cuisines classiques
Klassische Küchen
CLASSICAL KITCHENS
Cocinas clásicas

Classical style kitchens are defined by their precise aesthetic, with modules in the upper and lower parts of the work zone and paneled cabinet doors. Light-toned woods help to recreate a style which respects tradition. It is important not to overload the area, since the kitchen should be, above all, a very practical and comfortable space so as to be able to work freely. Solid wood cabinets may be elected, though veneered furnishings are more common in kitchens given the fact that they are lighter and more economical. Nowadays, purely classical modules with an elegant aesthetic are manufactured, though more contemporary designs may also be included in this style. Among these types of kitchens, the ones that utilize very innovative materials stand out for the incorporation of very light-colored materials (e.g., white veneers and laminations) or the combination with glass. Cabinets with shelves and glass enhance this style, as do paneled doors. Coverings for floors and walls are very useful in defining the classical style of a kitchen. The use of light-toned wooden slats for floor surfaces and ceramic tiles for walls offer very good results. A marble or granite countertop gives the work zone a classical and elegant appearance. Classical sinks, fixtures and extractor hoods highlight this style, as do domestic appliances of sober and discreet line. Luminous materials are good for the utility room, the walls of which may be painted with light colors and covered with wallpaper. Even decorative friezes are an option.

Cuisines classiques
Klassische Küchen
CLASSICAL KITCHENS
Cocinas clásicas

Charakteristisch für Küchen im klassischen Stil ist ein sehr solides und qualitativ hochwertiges Design, oben wie unten im Arbeitsbereich geprägt durch Schrankelemente, die Flügeltüren haben können. Entscheidet man sich für diesen traditionsverbundenen Stil, so ist helles Holz eine gute Wahl. Wichtig ist, dass der Raum nicht überladen wird, denn die Küche sollte vor allem sehr praktisch und bequem sein, um ungehindert darin arbeiten zu können. Schränke aus Massivholz stellen eine Möglichkeit dar, doch am häufigsten findet man in diesen Küchen Möbel mit Holzfurnier, die leichter und preiswerter sind. Gegenwärtig werden streng klassische, sehr elegante Modelle hergestellt, wenngleich diesem Stil auch zeitgenössischere Projekte zugeordnet werden können. Auffällig an diesen Küchen, bei denen ganz innovative Materialien verwendet werden, sind der Einsatz sehr heller Materialien (wie weiße Furniere und Beschichtungen) oder Verbindungen von hellem Holz mit hellen Materialien bzw. Kombinationen mit Glas. Unterstrichen wird dieser Stil durch Schränke mit Regalen und Vitrinen oder Flügeltüren. Auch Verkleidungen von Böden und Wänden eignen sich sehr gut, um den klassischen Stil einer Küche zu betonen. Die Verwendung heller Holzlatten für den Bodenbelag führen zu sehr guten Ergebnissen ebenso wie helle Fliesen an den Wänden. Eine Auflage aus Marmor oder Granit verleiht dem Arbeitsbereich einen Hauch von klassischer Eleganz. Unterstützung findet der Stil ebenfalls in streng traditionellen Spülbecken, Armaturen und Dunstabzugshauben sowie in nüchternen Haushaltsgeräten in schlichtem Design. Hinsichtlich des Mobiliars im Essbereich können helle Materialien gewählt werden; für die Wände reichen die Alternativen von einem hellen Anstrich über farbige Tapeten bis hin zu Zierleisten.

Cuisines classiques
Classical Kitchens
KLASSISCHE KÜCHEN
Cocinas clásicas

Les cuisines de style classique ont une esthétique très soignée, avec des modules installés dans la partie supérieure et inférieure du plan de travail, et des portes d'armoires à panneaux. Les bois clairs aident à recréer ce style qui respecte la tradition. Il est important de ne pas surcharger cette pièce, du fait que la cuisine doit être avant tout un endroit très pratique et agréable où l'on peut travailler librement. On peut choisir des armoires de bois massif bien que dans la cuisine, le plus courant soit des meubles en plaqué qui sont plus légers et économiques. Actuellement on fabrique des modèles purement classiques, avec une esthétique très élégante. On peut pourtant intégrer d'autres idées plus modernes dans ce style. Ce type de cuisine, qui utilise des matériaux très innovateurs, se distingue en intégrant des pièces très claires (comme du plaqué ou du laminé blanc), ou en réalisant des combinaisons de bois avec d'autres matériaux claires ou du verre. Ce style vient rehaussé avec des armoires à étagères, à vitrines, ou qui ont des portes à panneaux. Les revêtements des sols et des parois sont des éléments utiles pour définir le style classique d'une cuisine. On obtient de bon résultats en mettant un parquet de bois claire ainsi qu'en utilisant une faïence claire pour les parois. Une surface de travail en marbre ou en granit lui donne un aspect antique et élégant à la fois. Les éviers, la robinetterie et les hottes d'aspiration classiques rehaussent ce style de même que les appareils électro-ménagers qui ont des lignes sobres et discrètes. Pour le mobilier de l'office, on peut choisir des matériaux lumineux, peindre les parois de couleurs claires, les revêtir de papier peint ou y mettre des bordures décoratives.

Classical Kitchens

Klassische Küchen

CUISINES CLASSIQUES

Cocinas clásicas

Las cocinas de estilo clásico se definen por tener una estética muy cuidada, con módulos en la zona superior e inferior de la zona de trabajo y puertas de armarios con cuarterones. La madera en tonos claros es una buena opción para recrear este estilo que respeta la tradición. Es importante no cargar excesivamente la estancia, puesto que la cocina debe ser, ante todo, un espacio muy práctico y cómodo para poder trabajar libremente. Pueden elegirse armarios de madera maciza, aunque lo más habitual en la cocina son los muebles chapados, más ligeros y económicos. En la actualidad se fabrican modelos totalmente clásicos con una estética muy elegante, aunque también pueden incluirse en este estilo proyectos más actuales. Este tipo de cocinas, que utiliza materiales muy innovadores, destaca por su claridad (con chapados y laminados en blanco) y por realizar combinaciones de madera clara y materiales claros o combinados con cristal. Realzan este estilo armarios con estanterías y vitrinas, o puertas con postigos. Los revestimientos para suelos y paredes son elementos muy útiles para definir el estilo clásico de una cocina. Emplear lamas de madera clara en el suelo y azulejos de tonos pastel en las paredes da muy buenos resultados. Una encimera de mármol o granito aporta a la zona de trabajo un aspecto antiguo a la vez que elegante. Los fregaderos, griferías y campanas extractoras en su versión más clásica realzan este estilo, igual que los electrodomésticos de líneas sobrias y discretas. Para el mobiliario del office pueden elegirse materiales luminosos, pintar las paredes de colores claros, revestirlas con papel pintado e incluso colocarles cenefas decorativas.

Cuisines
classiques
Klassische Küchen
COCINAS
CLÁSICAS
*Classical
Kitchens*

Un classique modernisé
Modernisierter Klassiker
MODERN CLASSIC
Un clásico actualizado

Tradition sur petite surface
Tradition auf kleinem Raum
TRADITION IN SMALL SPACE
Tradición en pocos metros

Brillant naturel
Natürlicher Glanz
NATURAL SHINE
Brillo natural

De couleur crème
Cremefarben
CREAM COLOR
De color crema

Ciel bleu
Blauer Himmel
BLUE SKY
Cielo azul

Très bien équipée
Gut ausgestattet
WELL EQUIPPED
Muy bien equipada

De formes élégantes
Elegante Formen
ELEGANT FORMS
Formas elegantes

Ouverte sur le salon
Offen zum Salon
OPEN TO SALON
Abierta al salón

Photo © Nuria Fuentes

Répartition sage
Weise Aufteilung

Architect: **Francisco de la Guardia**

WISE DISTRIBUTION
Sabia distribución

Photo © Jordi Miralles

185

Cuisines rustiques
Rustikale Küchen
RUSTIC KITCHENS
Cocinas rústicas

Rustic kitchens recreate a rural and natural living style. Solid wood fittings of natural color or darker tones are most appropriate for this type of kitchen, though veneered fittings are used more often nowadays. Also appropriate are furnishings painted blue, white and green. Rustic cabinet doors include panels covered in wood, glass or chicken wire. Another good option are work pieces in the lower areas of the kitchen, typical in rural homes, which may be decorated with restored doors or checkered curtains with flounces. With regard to coverings, good ideas for the walls are utilizing white ceramic tile, restoring stone or brick walls, or applying paints that offer an irregular finish. Old-style kitchens in which half of the wall was tiled so as to cover the work zone (the area exposed to the most wear and tear) and the rest painted may also be imitated. For floors, clay tiles or wide wooden slats are ideal. Restored wooden beams, even painted, are good for ceilings. There is a variety of antique furniture that fits in perfectly with this type of kitchen: work tables (large tables used to prepare meals), auction cupboards (large glass cupboards to store crockery), brass handles or old fixtures that can be combined with porcelain details. Today, many kitchens combine antique elements and cutting edge fittings with aesthetically pleasing results. Details such as old decorative guides with saucepans and pans, shelves with spice bottles, or wicker boxes contribute to achieving the necessary warmth.

Cuisines rustiques
Rustikale Küchen
RUSTIC KITCHENS
Cocinas rústicas

Als rustikale Küchen bezeichnet man jene, die einen ländlichen und natürlichen Lebensstil nachempfinden. Am geeignetsten sind hierzu Möbel aus naturbelassenem Massivholz oder in dunklerer Färbung, wenngleich gegenwärtig Furniere stärker zum Einsatz kommen. Ebenfalls geeignet sind blau, weiß oder grün gestrichene Küchenmöbel. Charakteristisch für rustikale Schränke sind Flügeltüren mit Füllungen aus Holz, Glas oder Maschendraht. Eine andere gute Möglichkeit stellen Einbaumöbel im unteren Bereich der Küche dar, wie sie für Landhäuser typisch sind, dekoriert mit alten Türen, die hier eine neue Verwendung finden, oder mit karierten Gardinen mit Rüschen. Hinsichtlich der Verkleidung ist es bei Wänden empfehlenswert, weiße Fliesen zu wählen, Stein- oder Ziegelwänden ihre alte Schönheit wiederzugeben oder Farben für ungleichmäßige Oberflächen zu verwenden. Es können auch Küchen von früher imitiert werden, in denen die Wände bis auf halbe Höhe gefliest wurden (wodurch der Arbeitsbereich, in dem die Abnutzung am größten ist, geschützt wurde) und der Rest der Wand einen Farbanstrich erhielt. Ideal für den Bodenbelag sind Fließen aus Terrakotta oder Zement sowie breite Holzlatten. An der Decke schließlich findet man freigelegte Balken eventuell sogar mit Malereien. Es gibt alte Möbel, die perfekt in diese Art Küche passen: Hier finden auf Versteigerungen erworbene Arbeitstische oder Wandschränke eine neue Bestimmung, ebenso wie Messinggriffe und alte Armaturen, die mit Porzellanelementen kombiniert werden können. Heutzutage erzielt man in vielen Küchen durch ein Nebeneinander von alten Elementen und avantgardistischen Möbeln einen sehr ansprechenden Effekt. Details wie alte Zierleisten mit Töpfen und Pfannen, Regale mit Gewürzgläsern oder Behältnisse aus Korb tragen zu einer angemessenen warmen Ausstrahlung bei.

Cuisines rustiques
Rustic Kitchens
RUSTIKALE KÜCHEN
Cocinas rústicas

Les cuisines rustiques recréent le style de vie naturel et campagnard. Les meubles les plus appropriés sont en bois massifs de couleur naturelle ou éventuellement d'un ton un peu plus foncé. Aujourd'hui on utilise de plus en plus du plaqué. Les meubles de cuisines peints en vert, en blanc ou en bleu sont aussi très appropriés. Les portes d'armoires rustiques ont des panneaux de bois, de verre ou a croisillons. Un autre choix judicieux étant les meubles de cuisine bas, typiques dans les cuisines de campagne, décorés de portes antiques restaurées ou de rideaux à carreaux avec des volants. Quand aux revêtements, le carrelage blanc représente l'une des meilleures solutions de même que des parois restaurées de pierre ou de brique ou des peintures ayant une structure irrégulière. On peut également recréer des cuisines antiques en posant des carreaux sur une partie des parois ainsi que sur le plan de travail (très exposé à l'usure), et peindre le reste. Pour le sol, les dalles de terre cuite sont idéales ainsi que de larges planches de bois ou du carrelage. De vielles poutres de bois restaurées ou même peintes sont bien pour le plafond. Il y a des meubles antiques qui s'intègrent à la perfection à ce type de cuisines : de vieilles tables de cuisine (qui sont de grande taille et sur lesquelles ont préparait les repas), ou des dressoirs (grands buffets à vitrines ou l'on range la vaisselle), ainsi que des poignées de laiton et des robinets anciens pouvant être combinés avec des détails en porcelaine. De nos jours on aime beaucoup combiner des éléments antiques à un mobilier d'avant-garde, ce qui donne souvent des résultats admirables. Des détails tels que des tringles antiques pour suspendre casseroles et poêles, des petites étagères à épices ou des corbeilles d'osier contribuent à obtenir la chaleur requise.

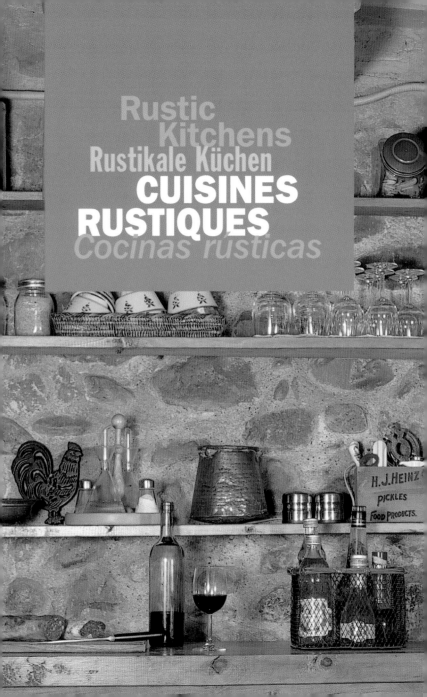

Rustic Kitchens

Rustikale Küchen

CUISINES RUSTIQUES

Cocinas rústicas

Las cocinas rústicas son las que recrean el estilo de vida campestre y natural. Los muebles más apropiados son los de madera maciza en color natural o incluso de un tono más oscuro, aunque en la actualidad se utilizan más los chapados. También son apropiados los muebles de cocina en azul, blanco y verde. Las puertas de armarios rústicos incorporan cuarterones, cubiertos con madera, cristal o tela de gallinero. Otra buena opción son los muebles de obra situados en los bajos de la cocina, típicos de las casas de campo y que pueden decorarse con puertas antiguas recuperadas o bien incorporando cortinas de cuadros con volantes. En cuanto a los revestimientos, una buena opción para las paredes es elegir azulejos blancos, recuperar las paredes de piedra o de ladrillo o utilizar pinturas que ofrecen acabados irregulares. También pueden imitarse las antiguas cocinas en las que se alicataba media pared de azulejos (que cubría la zona de trabajo, que es la de mayor desgaste) y se pintaba el resto de la pared. Para el pavimento, resulta ideal un suelo de barro cocido, lamas anchas de madera o bien azulejos. Y para el techo, vigas recuperadas de madera o incluso pintadas. Hay muebles antiguos que encajan a la perfección con este tipo de cocinas: recuperar mesas tocineras (mesas muy grandes que se utilizaban para preparar los alimentos) o alacenas de almoneda (grandes vitrinas para almacenar la vajilla), así como tiradores de latón y griferías antiguas, que pueden combinarse con detalles de porcelana. En la actualidad, muchas cocinas combinan elementos antiguos con muebles vanguardistas; es una mezcla que da resultados muy vistosos. Detalles como guías decorativas antiguas con cazos y sartenes, estanterías con botes de especias o cajas de mimbre contribuyen a conseguir la calidez necesaria.

Cuisines
rustiques
Rustikale Küchen
COCINAS
RÚSTICAS
Rustic Kitchens

Inspiration rustique
Rustikale Inspiration
RUSTIC INSPIRATION
Inspiración rústica

Cuisine personnelle
Persönliche Küche
PERSONAL KITCHEN
Cocina personal

La saveur de la tradition
Geschmack an Tradition
TASTE OF TRADITION
El sabor de la tradición

Architect: **Joan Bach**

Un classique élégant
Klassische Eleganz
CLASSIC ELEGANCE
Un clásico elegante

Design by: **Massimo Iosa Ghini**

Cuisine vert
Küche in Grün
GREEN KITCHEN
Cocina verde

Cuisine méditerranée
Mediterrane Küche
MEDITERRANEAN KITCHEN
Cocina mediterránea

Passé modernise
Moderne Vergangenheit
MODERN PAST
Pasado actual

Vivre dans la cuisine
Wohnen in der Küche
LIVING IN THE KITCHEN
Viviendo en la cocina

Photo © Jordi Miralles

221

Cuisines modernes et avant-gardistes

Moderne und avantgardistische Küchen

MODERN AND AVANT-GARDE KITCHENS

Cocinas actuales y vanguardistas

These are the most up-to-date kitchens, with varied but common design objectives: lightness, easy-use, and accessibility. New kitchens opt for functional elements, making them practical spaces with a rational distribution based on the differentiation of use. There are modules created exclusively for the cooking zone, the work zone, the pantry zone, or the storage area. Each zone may function independently, though all of them should be integrated with the entire kitchen ensemble. There is a wide range of designs on the market: ones with a retro tendency, ones of simple and pure line, or ones of industrial conception. Each kitchen acquires its own personality, and for this reason contemporary kitchen style incorporates a multitude of alternatives. Some options combine the most innovative materials while others tend toward more traditional materials. While many interior designers opt for light colors and the aesthetic of metallic materials such as stainless steel (which add luster and luminosity to the space), there are those who prefer bolder designs with colors such as red, intense yellow or blue or dark wood fittings such as wengué. One of the essential characteristics of the contemporary home is the practicality of its elements. In many cases the kitchen is a kind of living room or an open area with a table that may serve for meals, studying or work. Large spaces with an area reserved for the utility room or smaller kitchens in which the work area becomes a practical area for breakfasting are only some of the designs available for this room geared towards comfort, where originality is not reined in by merely practical function.

Cuisines modernes et avant-gardistes
Moderne und avantgardistische Küchen
MODERN AND AVANT-GARDE KITCHENS
Cocinas actuales y vanguardistas

Bei avantgardistischen Küchen handelt es sich um zeitgenössische Küchen von unterschiedlichstem Design, die jedoch stets folgende Gemeinsamkeiten haben: Dynamik, Leichtigkeit, unkomplizierte Nutzung und Zugänglichkeit. Moderne Küchen werden durch funktionale Elemente in praktische Räume mit einer äußerst rationalen Aufteilung verwandelt, die sich aus ihrer differenzierten Nutzung ergibt. Jeder Bereich ist weitgehend unabhängig funktionsfähig, muss allerdings in den Küchenkomplex insgesamt integriert sein. Der Markt bietet eine Vielzahl von Designs: im Retrotrend, mit schlichten, klaren Linien oder nach industriellem Vorbild. Jede Küche erhält ihre eigene Persönlichkeit, sodass der zeitgenössische Stil eine breite Palette von Möglichkeiten bietet: Werden hier innovativste Materialien kombiniert, so bevorzugt man dort die traditionelleren. Obschon viele Innenarchitekten auf helle Farben und metallische Materialien wie Edelstahl (der dem Raum Licht und Glanz verleiht) setzen, tendieren andere zu gewagteren Designs mit Farben wie z. B. Rot, kräftigem Gelb oder Blau oder zu Möbeln aus dunklem Holz wie Wengué. Eine der Haupteigenschaften moderner Wohnungen ist der praktische Charakter ihrer Elemente. Als Küchen bevorzugt man heutzutage häufig Wohn- oder offene Küchen mit einem Tisch, der sowohl zum Essen als auch zum Studieren oder Arbeiten genutzt werden kann. Große Räume mit einem dem Essbereich vorbehaltenen Teil oder kleinere Küchen, in denen sich der Arbeitsbereich in einen nützlichen Frühstückstisch verwandelt, sind nur eine kleine Auswahl der in diese Rubrik fallenden Möglichkeiten, bei denen die Bequemlichkeit im Mittelpunkt steht und sich Originalität und rein praktische Funktion nicht widersprechen.

Cuisines modernes et avant-gardistes
Modern and Avant-garde Kitchens
MODERNE UND AVANTGARDISTISCHE KÜCHEN
Cocinas actuales y vanguardistas

Ce sont les cuisines modernes de designs très variés, ayant comme objectifs communs : Dynamisme, légèreté, facilité d'usage, accessibilité. Elles ont des éléments fonctionnels qui les convertissent en espaces pratiques, avec une répartition rationnelle basée sur la différentiation des usages. Il existe ainsi des modules créés uniquement pour la zone de cuisson, de travail, de l'office ou du garde-manger. Chaque zone peut fonctionner avec une indépendance suffisante tout en étant intégrée au reste de la cuisine. Le marché propose une grande variété de design : de tendances rétro, de lignes pures et simples, de conception industrielle. Chaque cuisine acquière une personnalité propre, du fait que le style actuel offre un grand éventail de possibilités : certaines combinent les matériaux les plus innovateurs, d'autres préfèrent des matériaux plus traditionnels. Bien que beaucoup d'architectes d'intérieur misent sur des couleurs claires et sur une esthétique de matériaux métalliques comme l'acier inoxydable (qui donne du brillant et de la luminosité à l'espace, il en existe qui préfèrent des designs plus osés avec des couleurs rouges, jaunes intense ou bleues ou un mobilier de bois foncé comme le wengué. Une des caractéristiques essentielle des demeures actuelles est qu'elles ont des éléments pratiques. Dans beaucoup de cas, la cuisine est de type living et ouverte, avec une table pouvant servir à manger, à travailler ou à étudier. De grands espaces avec une zone réservée à l'office, ou des cuisines plus petites dans lesquelles la zone de travail peut être convertie en zone pour le petit déjeuner, ne sont que quelques propositions offertes par ce genre ouvert à la commodité et où l'originalité n'est pas restreinte à la fonction purement pratique.

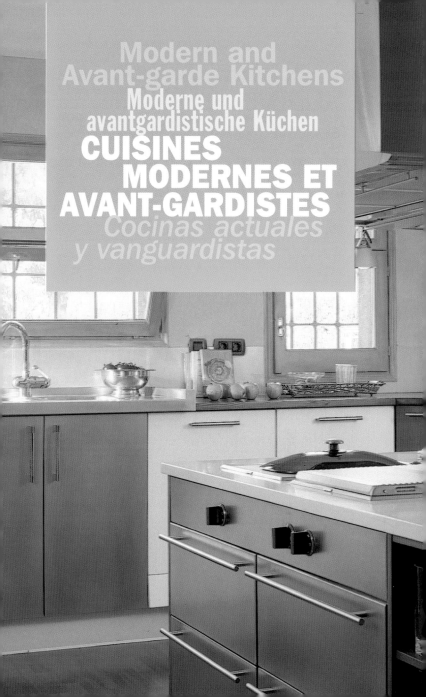

Modern and Avant-garde Kitchens
Moderne und avantgardistische Küchen
CUISINES MODERNES ET AVANT-GARDISTES
Cocinas actuales y vanguardistas

Son las cocinas actuales, de diseño muy variado aunque con objetivos comunes: dinamismo, ligereza, facilidad de uso y accesibilidad. Las nuevas cocinas apuestan por elementos funcionales que las convierten en espacios prácticos, con una distribución muy racional basada en la diferenciación de los usos. Así, existen módulos creados únicamente para la zona de cocción, otros sólo para la zona de trabajo y otros para la de despensa o almacenamiento. Cada zona puede funcionar con suficiente independencia, aunque deben estar integradas en el conjunto de la cocina. En el mercado existe gran variedad de diseños: de tendencias "revival", de líneas simples y puras, de concepción industrial... cada cocina adquiere personalidad propia, por lo que el estilo actual es un gran abanico de opciones: algunas combinan los materiales más innovadores, mientras que otras prefieren los más tradicionales. Aunque muchos interioristas apuestan por los colores claros y por la estética de los materiales metalizados como el acero inoxidable (que dota al espacio de brillo y luminosidad), hay quien apuesta por diseños más atrevidos, con colores como el rojo, el amarillo intenso o el azul, o por mobiliario de maderas oscuras como el wengué. Una de las características esenciales de las viviendas actuales es la practicidad de sus elementos. En muchos casos, la cocina actual es tipo living o abierta, con una mesa que bien puede servir para las comidas, para el estudio o el trabajo. Espacios grandes con una zona reservada al office o cocinas más pequeñas en las que la zona de trabajo se convierte en una útil barra de desayuno son algunas de las propuestas que se incluyen en este apartado abierto a la comodidad, donde la originalidad no está reñida con la función meramente práctica.

Cuisines modernes et avant-gardistes
Moderne und avantgardistische Küchen
COCINAS ACTUALES Y VANGUARDISTAS
Modern and Avant-garde Kitchens

Esthétique Zen
Zen Ästhetik
ZEN AESTHETIC
Estética zen

L'espace ouvert
Offener Raum
OPEN SPACE
Espacio abierto

Design by: **Elmar Cucine**

Contours multicolores
Bunte Kurven
MULTICOLORED CURVES
Curvas multicolores

Idée originale
Originelle Idee
ORIGINAL IDEA
Idea original

Rose et rouge
Rosa und Rot
PINK AND RED
Rosa y rojo

251

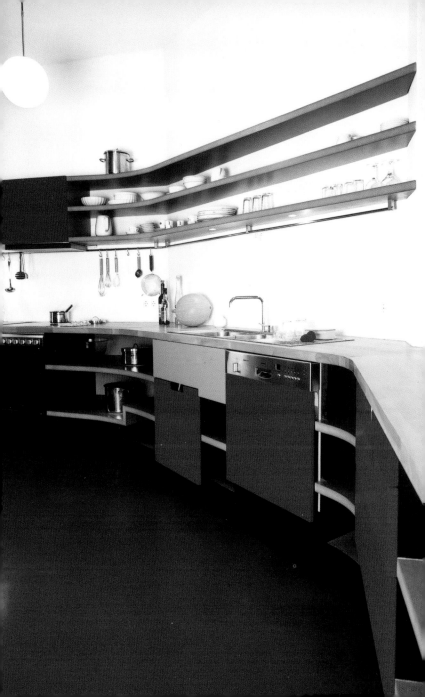

Espace pour en profiter

Viel Platz zum Genießen

A LARGE SPACE TO ENJOY

Espacio para disfrutar

Design by: **Massimo Iosa Ghini**

Un loft intelligent
Intelligentes Loft
INTELLIGENT LOFT
Un loft inteligente

Fonctions multiples
Multifunktional
MULTIPLE
FUNCTIONS
Múltiples funciones

Photo © Jordi Miralles

263

Continuité visuelle
Visuelle Kontinuität
VISUAL CONTINUITY
Continuidad visual

SMALL DIMENSIONS

Petites dimensions
Kleine Dimensionen
Pequeñas dimensiones

Comme un couloir
Wie ein Korridor
LIKE A CORRIDOR
Como un pasillo

Avec vue
Mit Aussicht
WITH VIEW
Design by: **Massimo Iosa Ghini**
Con vistas

Grande zone de travail

Eine große Arbeitsfläche

Architect: **Roger Bellera**

AN EXTENSIVE WORKING AREA

Gran zona de trabajo

Photo © Jordi Miralles

Ondes singulières
Einzelne Wellen
SINGULAR WAVES
Ondas singulares

Design by: **Massimo Iosa Ghini**

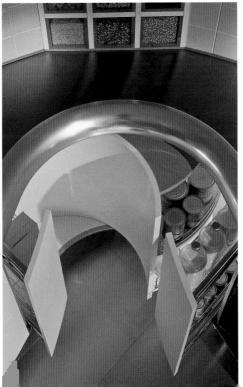

Cuisines minimalistes
Minimalistische Küchen
MINIMALISTIC KITCHENS
Cocinas minimalistas

Of pure conception and eclectic style, minimalistic kitchens are noteworthy for occupying a single space in original environments without ornamental frills. Their clean and ordered forms constitute in themselves a decorative function. This type of kitchen tends to appear in new-style homes such as lofts or small studios in which the kitchen seeks to establish a unifying dialogue with the other areas of the home. They are kitchens of refined design, conceived to be functional while at the same time spectacular. Sometimes one wall contains all cabinets and kitchen elements thanks to an intelligent arrangement. Other times a single elongated module (island-fashion without separations) includes the kitchen, with all necessities reduced to a minimum of expression. In still another instance the kitchen shares space with the dining room and living room, requiring a rational, well-thought-out spatial arrangement. In homes without walls the kitchen may be separated from the other rooms by panels of medium height. With regard to location, especially if the kitchen joins with other environments, furnishings in accord with the general decoration are required: light-toned furniture or dark cabinets to match the living room design are two possibilities. Some minimalist kitchens adapt to unconventional architectures, taking advantage of difficult angles, narrow corridors, or even sharing the same room with more than one environment. In minimalist kitchens the selection of contemporary materials for coverings and countertops combines with state-of-the-art domestic appliances to create an environment in which order and functionality are the two essential elements.

Cuisines
minimalistes
Minimalistische
Küchen

MINIMALISTIC KITCHENS

Cocinas
minimalistas

Klar im Entwurf und stilistisch ausgewogen, ist für minimalistische Küchen vor allem ein außergewöhnlicher Raum mit origineller Atmosphäre und ohne schmückende Elemente charakteristisch. Ihre reinen und übersichtlichen Formen selbst erfüllen bereits eine dekorative Funktion. Gewöhnlich wird dieser Küchentyp für moderne Wohnungen im Loftstil oder kleine Apartments entworfen, in denen die Formensprache der anderen Wohnungsbereiche durch die Küche wieder aufgenommen werden soll. Es handelt sich um Küchen von ausgefeiltem Design mit dem Anspruch, funktional und Aufsehen erregend zugleich zu sein. Mitunter nimmt eine einzige Wand dank einer intelligenten Aufteilung sämtliche Schränke und Küchenelemente auf. In anderen Fällen beinhaltet ein einziges lang gestrecktes Modul die auf das absolute Minimum reduzierte Küche mit allem Notwendigen (im Stile einer Insel, ohne Unterteilungen). Oder die Küche teilt sich den Raum mit dem Essoder gar dem Wohnzimmer, was eine rationale, sehr wohl durchdachte Aufteilung erfordert. In wandlosen Wohnungen können die Küche und die übrigen Räume durch halbhohe Paneele abgetrennt werden. Je nach Lage der Küche – vor allem, wenn sie in andere Bereichen integriert wird – ist auf Mobiliar zu achten, das sich in die allgemeine Ausstattung einfügt: Denkbar sind hier Möbel in hellen Tönen oder auch dunkle Schränke, passend zum Mobiliar des Wohnzimmers. Teilweise werden minimalistische Küchen an extreme Grundrisse angepasst, indem schwierige Winkel oder enge Gänge ausgenutzt werden oder der Raum mehr als nur einen Bereich aufnimmt. Neben modernen Materialien für Verkleidungen und Arbeitsplatten finden sich Hightech-Hausgeräte, speziell ausgewählt für diese Art von Küche, in der Ordnung und Funktionalität oberstes Kriterium sind.

Cuisines minimalistes
Minimalistic Kitchens
MINIMALISTISCHE KÜCHEN
Cocinas minimalistas

De conception pure et de style éclectique, les cuisines minimalistes se définissent en occupant un espace propre dans un environnement original et sans ornements. Ses formes propres et ordonnées ont une fonction décorative en soit. On trouve le plus souvent ce type de cuisine dans les appartements du type « loft », ou dans des petits studios dans lesquels la cuisine essaie d'établir un dialogue pour l'unir avec le reste de la maison. Elles ont un design dépouillé, pensé pour être fonctionnel et spectaculaire à la fois. Parfois, une seule paroi peut loger, grâce à une répartition intelligente, toutes les armoires et éléments de la cuisine. D'autres fois, un unique module allongé (genre îlot, sans séparations), contient la cuisinière et tout ce qui est nécessaire réduit à un minimum. Dans d'autres cas, la cuisine se partage un espace avec la salle à manger et même avec le salon, ce qui nécessite une répartition rationnelle très bien pensée. Pour les logements n'ayant pas de parois, la cuisine et les autres espaces peuvent être séparés au moyen de panneaux à mi-hauteur. En fonction de son emplacement et surtout si on l'intègre aux autres espaces, elle requière un type de mobilier qui s'adapte à la décoration générale : meubles aux tons claires ou armoires foncées en relation avec le mobilier du salon sont quelques unes des options. Certaines cuisines minimaliste s'adaptent à un architecture extrême, permettant d'utiliser les angles difficiles, des passages étroits ou en donnant à une pièce différentes atmosphères. Un choix de matériaux modernes pour le revêtement et les surfaces de travail combinés aux appareils électro-ménagers de la dernière génération sont employés pour ce type de cuisines dans lesquelles l'ordre et la fonctionnalité sont les deux éléments primordiaux.

Minimalistic
Kitchens
Minimalistische Küchen
CUISINES
MINIMALISTES
Cocinas
minimalistas

De concepción pura y estilo ecléctico, las cocinas minimalistas se definen por ocupar un espacio singular en ambientes originales y sin elementos ornamentales. Sus formas limpias y ordenadas establecen ya una función decorativa por sí mismas. Este tipo de cocinas suele proyectarse en las nuevas viviendas tipo loft o en estudios pequeños en los que la cocina pretende establecer un lenguaje de unión con los demás compartimentos de la casa. Son cocinas de diseño depurado, pensadas para ser funcionales y espectaculares a la vez. A veces una única pared alberga, gracias una inteligente distribución, todos los armarios y elementos de la cocina. Otras veces, un único módulo alargado (a modo de isla, sin separaciones) incluye la cocina, con todo lo necesario reducido a la mínima expresión. En otros casos, la cocina comparte espacio con el comedor e incluso con el salón, por lo que requiere de una distribución muy racional. Para las viviendas que no utilizan paredes, la cocina y los otros espacios pueden separarse mediante paneles a media altura. En función de su ubicación, sobre todo si se integran en otros ambientes, requieren de un tipo de mobiliario que se adapte a la decoración general: muebles de tonos claros o bien armarios oscuros, a juego con el mobiliario del salón, son algunas de las opciones. Algunas cocinas minimalistas se adaptan a arquitecturas extremas, aprovechando ángulos difíciles, pasillos estrechos o bien compartiendo una misma estancia con más de un ambiente. La elección de materiales actuales para revestimientos y encimeras combina con los electrodomésticos de última generación en estas cocinas cuyos elementos primordiales son el orden y la funcionalidad.

Cuisines minimalistes
Minimalistische Küchen
COCINAS MINIMALISTAS
Minimalistic Kitchens

Grande capacité
Große Kapazität
BIG CAPACITY
Gran capacidad

Photo © Montse Garriga

Légère et spacieuse
Leicht und geräumig
LIGHT AND SPACIOUS
Ligera y espaciosa

Photo © Elmar Cucine

Formes simples
Einfache Formen
SIMPLE FORMS
Formas sencillas

Architect: **Kenji Hashimoto**

Photo © Nacása & Partners Inc.

Bleu marine
Marineblau
MARINE BLUE
Azul marino
Architect: **Brian Ma Siy**

L'art dans la cuisine
Kunst in der Küche
ART IN THE KITCHEN
Arte en la cocina

Ombres originales
Originelle Schatten
Architect: **Blockachitecture**
ORIGINAL SHADES
Originales sombras

Cuisines petites
Kleine Küchen
SMALL KITCHENS
Cocinas pequeñas

A small kitchen demands an intelligent arrangement in order to take maximum advantage of a limited amount of available space. It is thus essential to achieve practical angles, columns and corners. If a complete renovation is not possible, there are certain practical tricks that can be used. For example, sliding doors gain space and permit the unification or separation of environments, given the necessities of the moment. Shelves or small modules to store utensils may be placed in corners or "dead zones". Most important, the kitchen must always be organized and permit easy movement regardless of limited surface area. The type of fittings selected for this sort of kitchen is decisive. Utilizing customized furniture is a good solution. Selecting auxiliary modules or furniture pieces with wheels is also a versatile option given that they can be moved, thus allowing space to be opened up when necessary. These pieces may be placed below the worktable or utility-room table. The best alternative is to make use of walls to situate floor and ceiling cabinets (the latter may even reach the ceiling) in order to have enough storage space. Choosing light-colored furniture is wise for small kitchens, since they make the space seem larger. Any imaginative solution is appropriate, such as utilizing the space between steps in a set of stairs to store small items, hanging shelves from the ceiling to store cook books or work utensils, or making use of the kitchen sill for essentials while cooking. There are domestic appliances of reduced size, extensible extractor hoods that occupy little space, and sinks and fixtures of simple design, all of which are ideal for this type of kitchen.

Cuisines petites

Kleine Küchen

SMALL KITCHENS

Cocinas pequeñas

Kleine Küchen erfordern eine gute Aufteilung, um den wenigen verfügbaren Platz optimal zu nutzen. Deshalb ist es von grundlegender Bedeutung, Winkel, Säulen und Ecken günstig anzulegen. Falls ein umfangreicher Umbau nicht realisierbar ist, gibt es ein paar praktische, für diesen Küchentyp geeignete Tricks, wie z. B. den Einsatz von Schiebetüren, dank derer Raum gewonnen und eine Verbindung von Bereichen möglich wird. Umgekehrt können sie diese aber auch problemlos gemäß den jeweiligen Bedürfnissen trennen. Ecken oder tote Winkel können zum Aufstellen von Regalen oder kleinen Modulen genutzt werden, um Geräte aufzubewahren. Wichtig ist, dass die Küche trotz der kleinen Fläche stets aufgeräumt ist und Bewegungsfreiheit besteht. Die Auswahl des Mobiliars ist ein entscheidender Faktor bei diesem Küchentyp. Als günstig erweist sich der Einbau maßgefertigter Möbel oder man wählt ergänzende Module und Möbel mit Rädern, die je nach Bedarf verschoben oder unter dem Arbeits- oder Esstisch verstaut werden können. Am besten nutzt man die Wände zum Aufstellen von Unterschränken und Hängeschränken (die bis zur Decke reichen können), um genügend Stauraum zu schaffen. Ferner empfiehlt sich die Wahl von Möbeln in hellen Farben, weil sie den Raum optisch vergrößern helfen. Jede einfallsreiche Lösung ist willkommen: die Nutzung des Hohlraums von Treppenstufen zum Aufbewahren von kleinen Geräten; das Befestigen von Hängeregalen an der Decke, um Kochbücher und Arbeitsgegenstände abzustellen; oder die Benutzung des Fensterbretts in der Küche zum Abstellen der beim Kochen notwendigsten Dinge. Es gibt Haushaltsgeräte in kleinen Größen, ausziehbare Dunstabzugshauben, die kaum Platz einnehmen sowie Spülbecken und Armaturen von schlichtem Design, die für diese Art Küche ideale sind.

Cuisines
petites
Small Kitchens
KLEINE
KÜCHEN
Cocinas
pequeñas

Une cuisine de petite dimension exige une bonne répartition pour tirer le maximum de l'espace disponible. Des angles pratiques, des armoires et des coins bien pensés sont indispensables. Si une rénovation complète n'est pas possible, on peut employer quelques trucs pratiques qui s'adaptent à ce type de cuisine, tels que des portes coulissantes qui permettent de gagner de la place et réunissent ou séparent sans problèmes les espaces selon les besoins du moment. On peut utiliser les coins et les zones mortes pour mettre des étagères ou de petits modules destinés à ranger divers ustensiles. L'important est que même si la cuisine est petite, elle soit en ordre et qu'on puisse s'y déplacer aisément. Le mobilier choisit est décisif pour ce type de cuisine. L'utilisation de meubles sur mesure est une bonne option ainsi que de choisir des modules auxiliaire sur roues ce qui permet de les déplacer en fonction des espaces nécessités, de même qu'ils peuvent être placés sous les plans de travail ou dans l'office. Le mieux est d'utiliser les parois pour y placer des éléments bas et muraux (pouvant aller jusqu'au plafond) pour avoir suffisamment de capacité de rangement. Les meubles de cuisine de couleur claire sont idéals car ils font paraître la pièce plus grande. Toute solution ingénieuse est valable, comme, par exemple d'utiliser les espaces entre les marches d'une échelle pour ranger divers objets, suspendre des étagères au plafond pour y placer des livres de cuisine ou d'autres ustensiles de travail ou employer des rebords de fenêtre pour y déposer ce qui est utile pendant qu'on cuisine. Il existe des appareils électro-ménagers de petite taille, des hottes de ventilation extractibles occupant peu de place et des éviers et robinets d'un design simple idéals pour ce genre de cuisine.

Small Kitchens
Kleine Küchen
CUISINES PETITES
Cocinas
pequeñas

Una cocina de pocos metros exige una buena distribución para aprovechar al máximo el poco espacio disponible. Por ello, es elemental hacer prácticos ángulos, columnas y rincones. Si no puede hacerse una reforma a fondo, existen algunos trucos prácticos que se adaptan a este tipo de cocinas, como utilizar puertas correderas, que ganan espacio y permiten unificar ambientes o separarlos sin problemas en función de las necesidades del momento. Los rincones o zonas muertas pueden aprovecharse para colocar estanterías o módulos pequeños para almacenar utensilios. Lo importante es que, aunque no tenga muchos metros, la cocina esté siempre en orden y permita una fácil movilidad. El mobiliario elegido es un factor decisivo para este tipo de cocinas. La utilización de muebles a medida es una buena opción, así como elegir módulos o muebles auxiliares con ruedas, opción muy versátil que permite trasladarlos en función del espacio que se necesite, e incluso colocarlos debajo de la mesa de trabajo o del office. Lo mejor es aprovechar las paredes para colocar armarios inferiores y superiores (pueden llegar hasta el techo) para tener suficiente espacio de almacenamiento. Elegir los muebles de colores claros es una buena opción para cocinas reducidas, puesto que logran que el espacio se amplíe visualmente. Cualquier solución ingeniosa es válida, como utilizar el hueco de los peldaños de una escalera para almacenar pequeños enseres, colgar estantes suspendidos en el techo para depositar libros de cocina o utensilios de trabajo o aprovechar el antepecho de la cocina para colocar lo más necesario mientras se cocina. Existen electrodomésticos de tamaño reducido, campanas extractoras extensibles que casi no ocupan espacio y fregaderos y griferías de sencillos diseños, ideales para este tipo de cocinas.

Cuisines petites
Kleine Küchen
COCINAS ~PEQUEÑAS
Small Kitchens

Une cuisine de front

Frontale Küche

FRONTAL KITCHEN

Una cocina frontal

Photo © Montse Garriga

Bien répartie
Gut aufgeteilt
Architect: **Mr. Van der Meulen**
WELL DIVIDED
Bien compartido

Espace original
Origineller Raum
ORIGINAL SPACE
Espacio original

Cuisines industrielles
Großküchen
INDUSTRIAL KITCHENS
Cocinas industriales

Nowadays, the distinctive style of kitchens in public places such as large restaurants is being imitated in many domestic settings. These are roomy, practical, well-thought-out spaces in which spatial distribution is centered on the activities of preparing and cooking meals. Stainless steel is usually employed in this type of kitchen, as it may be cleaned easily and is highly resistant to water vapor and grease. The majority of industrial kitchens are manufactured exclusively with this material. These designs have been adopted primarily in private homes where the culinary art figures largely. Increasingly, companies are manufacturing stainless steel cabinets, countertops and hoods to match a gamut of up-to-date domestic appliances, sills and decorative elements. As a general rule, domestic appliances in this type of kitchen have a professional appearance and are of stainless steel to match the rest of the fitting. Contemporary industrial kitchens follow avant-garde guidelines in which the space dedicated to cooking opens up to the other rooms. The tendency is to leave the work zone open to view and not relegate it a secondary status. Some industrial kitchens, therefore, open to the restaurant with the aim of incorporating the preparation and enjoyment of meals in the same space. These kitchens incorporate refined designs with state-of-the-art materials that resist heat and chemical products. They are large, well-defined spaces with ample light. Distinct points of light in each zone allow one to work comfortably.

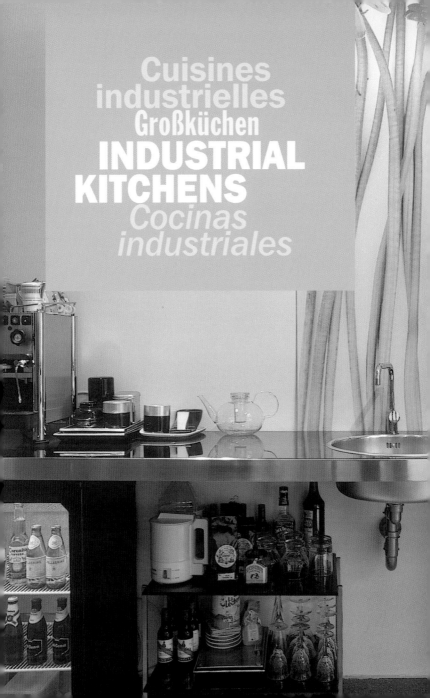

Cuisines industrielles
Großküchen
INDUSTRIAL KITCHENS
Cocinas industriales

Bei Küchen in öffentlichen Einrichtungen, z. B. in großen Restaurants, hat sich ein eigener Stil herausgebildet, der in vielen modernen Privatküchen imitiert wird. Charakteristisch sind weite und sehr praktische, gut durchdachte Räume, für deren Aufteilung die Vor- und Zubereitung der Lebensmittel die Richtschnur ist. Edelstahl ist das am häufigsten vorkommende Material in diesem Küchentyp, da er leicht zu reinigen und sehr widerstandsfähig gegen hohe Temperaturen, Wasserdampf und das beim Kochen auftretende Fett ist. Die Mehrzahl der Großküchen wird komplett aus Edelstahl hergestellt. Ihr Design wurde für die Privathaushalte angepasst – vor allem in jenen, in denen der Kochkunst große Bedeutung beigemessen wird. Es gibt immer mehr Hersteller, die Schränke, Arbeitsplatten und Frontpartien aus Edelstahl passend zu einer ganzen Palette aktueller Hausgeräte, Fensterbänke und dekorativer Elemente anbieten. Im Allgemeinen haben die Hausgeräte in dieser Art von Küchen ein professionelles Aussehen und sind, dem restlichen Mobiliar entsprechend, vorzugsweise aus Edelstahl. Heutige Großküchen folgen avantgardistischen Tendenzen, gemäß denen sich der Kochbereich den anderen Räumen öffnet. Der Trend geht dahin, den Arbeitsbereich dem Blick freizugeben und nicht in den Hintergrund zu drängen. So sind einige Großküchen zum Restaurant hin offen, um Zubereitung und Genuss der Speisen innerhalb desselben Raumes zu vereinen. Das Design ist ausgefeilt, die verwendeten Materialien sind beständig gegen Hitze und Chemikalien. Die großen Räume werden optimal genutzt und großzügig beleuchtet: Verschiedene, gut verteilte Lichtpunkte sorgen für ein bequemes Arbeiten in jedem Bereich.

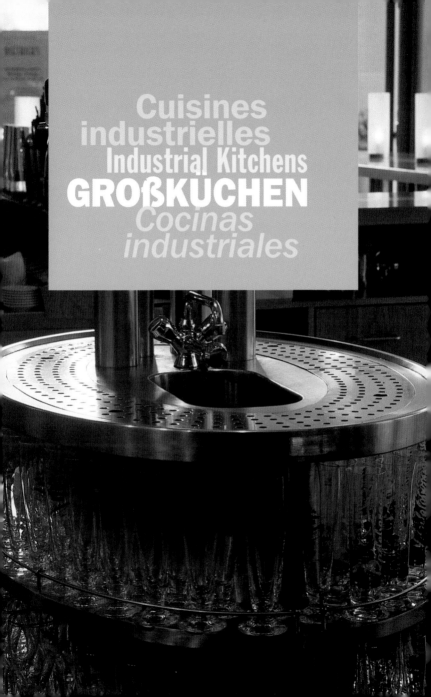

Cuisines
industrielles
Industrial Kitchens
GROßKUCHEN
*Cocinas
industriales*

Les cuisines de lieux publiques, comme les grands restaurants, ont un style propre, souvent imité dans les cuisines privées. Elles se définissent comme des espaces vastes, très pratiques et bien pensés, ayant une répartition centrée sur la préparation et la cuisson des aliments. L'acier inoxydable est le matériel le plus utilisé pour ce type de cuisines. Il se nettoie facilement et est très résistant à la chaleur, à l'eau, à la vapeur et aux graisses. La majorité des cuisines industrielles est fabriquée uniquement avec ce matériel. Ce design a été adopté largement dans les maisons particulières où l'art culinaire a pris de l'importance. De plus en plus de maisons fabriquent des armoires, des plans de travail et des parties frontales en acier inoxydable allant de paire avec toute une gamme d'électro-ménagers, de rebords et d'éléments de décoration. Les appareils électro-ménagers de ce type de cuisine adoptent un air professionnel et sont également en acier, en accord avec le reste du mobilier. Les cuisines industrielles modernes suivent les règles avant-gardistes en s'ouvrant sur d'autres pièces. La tendance est de laisser la vue sur la zone de travail au lieu de la reléguer au second plan. Ainsi certaines cuisines industrielles s'ouvrent sur le restaurant avec l'intention de réunir dans un même espace la préparation des aliments et leur dégustation. C'est un design dépouillé avec les matériaux de la dernière génération qui résistent à la chaleur et aux produits chimiques. De grands espaces bien aménagés ayant un éclairage généreux : des points de lumière bien répartis dans chacune des zones permettent de travailler commodément.

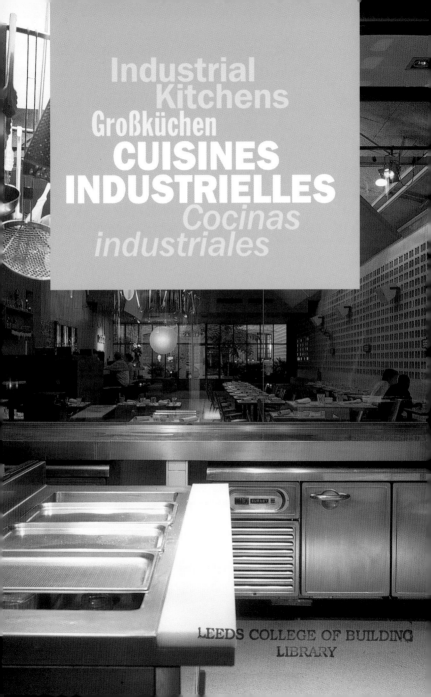

Industrial Kitchens
Kitchens
Großküchen
CUISINES INDUSTRIELLES
Cocinas industriales

Las cocinas de lugares públicos como grandes restaurantes han creado un estilo propio que se ha imitado en muchas cocinas privadas de construcción actual. Se definen por ser espacios amplios y muy prácticos, bien pensados, donde preparar y cocinar los alimentos se convierte en el eje fundamental de su distribución. El acero inoxidable es el material más utilizado en este tipo de cocinas, puesto que se limpia fácilmente y es muy resistente a las altas temperaturas, a los vapores de agua y a la grasa que se genera en la cocción: la mayoría de cocinas industriales se fabrica íntegramente con este material. Estos diseños se han adaptado a las viviendas familiares, sobre todo en aquellas en las que el arte culinario adquiere gran importancia. Cada vez son más las firmas que fabrican armarios, encimeras y frontales de acero inoxidable, a juego con toda una gama actual de electrodomésticos, antepechos y elementos decorativos. Por norma general, los electrodomésticos de este tipo de cocinas adoptan un aire profesional y se eligen en acero inoxidable, a juego con el resto del mobiliario. Las actuales cocinas industriales continúan las pautas vanguardistas, en que el espacio dedicado a cocinar se abre a otras estancias. La tendencia es dejar a la vista la zona de trabajo y no relegarla a un segundo término. Así, algunas cocinas industriales se abren al restaurante con la intención de compartir en un mismo espacio la preparación de los alimentos y la degustación de los mismos. Son diseños depurados, con materiales de última generación, resistentes al calor y a los productos químicos. Grandes espacios muy bien aprovechados y con una iluminación generosa: distintos puntos de luz bien distribuidos en cada una de las zonas para poder trabajar cómodamente.

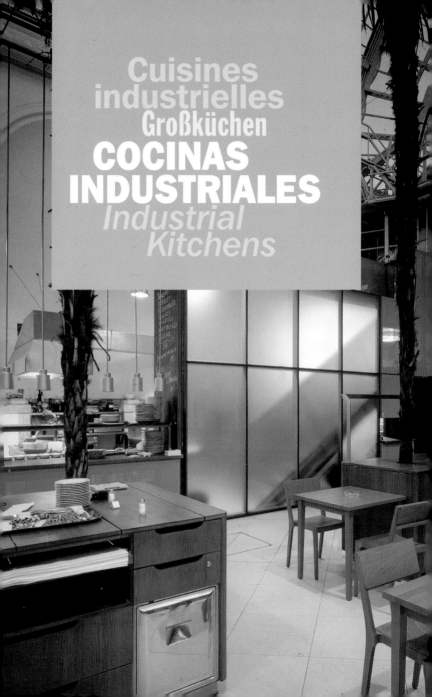

Cuisines industrielles
Großküchen
COCINAS INDUSTRIALES
Industrial Kitchens

Design exceptionnel
Einzigartiges Design
OUTSTANDING DESIGN
Diseño singular

Architect: **160BIS**

Retrouvant la tradition
Wiederfinden der Tradition
RECUPERATING TRADITION
Recuperando la tradición

Photo © Carlos Domínguez

Cuisines claires
Helle Küchen
BRIGHT
KITCHENS
Cocinas claras

Today, the kitchen is the center of family reunion, and as a result is often granted a prime placement in the house. In some cases it even occupies the center of the home. Some kitchens are very large and enjoy ample natural light, with windows to the outside or doors which communicate directly with a terrace. Yet, not all kitchens enjoy such a privileged location. For this reason there are solutions to help achieve a more luminous space. Knocking down partitions, building a kitchen-living room or a kitchen that opens to the living room are increasingly popular ways to benefit from the light entering adjacent rooms. If the kitchen is independent from the dining room, a window-like opening or sliding glass doors may be installed in order to unify the two zones and permit the passage of light. Selecting light-toned wood fittings, white, natural or beige cabinet faces, or combining them with glass are tricks to help make the kitchen seem less cumbersome and more luminous. Other solutions are light-structured tables, stools in place of large voluminous chairs, and domestic appliances of straight and discreet line. It is important not to crowd the space in order to have a functional, organized kitchen. If there is sufficient space, it is a good idea to place cabinets only in the lower part of the work zone. In this way the kitchen appears roomier. Situating a work island in the center of the room allows for the orderly distribution of each function. Good artificial lighting is imperative in order to be able to work comfortably when the sun goes down. It is thus important to have diverse points of light in each kitchen zone: general lighting in the ceiling, specific lighting in the cooking, work and pantry areas.

Cuisines claires
Helle Küchen
BRIGHT
KITCHENS
Cocinas claras

Die Küche ist heute Treffpunkt für die Familie, weshalb sie häufig in einer guten räumlichen Lage zu finden ist oder gar den Mittelpunkt der Wohnung bildet. Manche Küchen sind weiträumig, von Tageslicht durchflutet und verfügen über Fenster nach draußen oder Türen, die auf eine Terrasse führen. Nicht alle befinden sich in einem solch privilegierten Raum, doch gibt es für diese Lösungen, damit sie heller erscheinen. Der Abbruch von Zwischenwänden zur Vergrößerung des Raumes bzw. die Einrichtung von zum Wohnzimmer hin offenen Küchen ist ein immer häufiger gewählter Weg, um vom Licht umliegender Räume zu profitieren. Sind Küche und Esszimmer getrennt, kann eine Durchreiche angelegt werden oder man entscheidet sich für Glasschiebetüren zur Verbindung beider Räume und zur Gewährleistung des Lichtflusses. Die Wahl von Möbeln in hellen Hölzern oder solchen mit weißen, creme- oder beigefarbenen Frontpartien sowie die Kombination mit Glas sind Tricks, dank derer eine Küche leichter und heller wirkt. Zu den weiteren Möglichkeiten zählen leicht gebaute Tische, Hocker anstelle von großen, sperrigen Stühlen sowie Hausgeräte mit geraden, unauffälligen Linien. Es ist wichtig, den Raum nicht zu überladen – so entsteht eine funktionale und zugleich geordnete Küche. Steht genug Raum zur Verfügung, ist es sinnvoll, im Arbeitsbereich lediglich Unterschränke aufzustellen. Die Küche wirkt dadurch übersichtlicher. Das Einrichten einer Arbeitsinsel in der Mitte des Raumes erlaubt eine strukturierte Zuordnung der Bereiche für die jeweiligen Funktionen. Eine gute künstliche Beleuchtung ist unabdingbar, um nach Einbruch der Dunkelheit bequem arbeiten zu können. Wichtig sind daher verschiedene Lichtpunkte in sämtlichen Küchenbereichen: großflächiges Licht von der Decke und zielgerichtete Beleuchtung im Koch-, Arbeits- und Speisekammerbereich.

Cuisines claires
Bright Kitchens

HELLE KÜCHEN

Cocinas claras

Actuellement, la cuisine est le point de réunion de la famille. Elle dispose fréquemment d'un bon emplacement et se trouve en général au centre de la maison. Certaines cuisines sont grandes et disposent d'une lumière naturelle abondante, ayant des fenêtres sur l'extérieur ou des portes donnant sur la terrasse. Si elles ne jouissent pas d'un espace privilégié, il existe toujours une solution pour les faire paraître plus lumineuses. Abattre des cloisons ou construire une cuisine-living ou ouverte sur le salon sont des options de plus en plus courantes, qui permettent de profiter de la luminosité des pièces contiguës. Si la cuisine et la salle à manger sont séparées, on peut ouvrir un passe-plats, ou installer des portes coulissantes en verre ce qui les réunit et permet à la lumière de passer. Choisir un mobilier de bois clairs, des fronts d'armoires blancs, crus, beige ou les combiner à du verre, sont quelques trucs qui contribuent à faire paraître une cuisine plus légère et lumineuse. D'autres solutions sont d'y placer des tables de structure légère, de substituer des tabourets aux chaises qui sont plus grandes et volumineuses, et de choisir des électro-ménagers de lignes droites et discrètes. Il est nécessaire de ne pas surcharger l'espace, pour avoir une cuisine fonctionnelle et ordonnée. Si on a suffisamment de place, une bonne idée est, d'installer les meubles uniquement dans la partie inférieure, en dessous de la surface de travail. La cuisine paraîtra ainsi plus dégagée. Installer un îlot de travail au centre permet de faire une répartition très ordonnée des différentes zones. Un bon éclairage artificiel est indispensable pour pouvoir travailler convenablement lorsque le soleil disparaît. De ce fait il est important de disposer des points de lumière dans chacune des zones : éclairage général au plafond et points de lumière au dessus de la cuisinière, des surfaces de travail et dans le garde-manger.

Bright Kitchens
Helle Küchen
CUISINES
CLAIRES
Cocinas claras

En la actualidad, la cocina es el centro de reunión familiar, por lo que es frecuente que disponga de un buen emplazamiento e incluso que ocupe el centro de la vivienda. Algunas cocinas disponen de muchos metros y abundante luz natural, con ventanas al exterior o puertas que comunican directamente con la terraza. Sin embargo, no todas disfrutan de un espacio privilegiado, y por ello existen soluciones para conseguir que parezcan más luminosas. Derribar tabiques o construir una cocina living o abierta al salón son opciones cada vez más utilizadas para que se contagien de la luz de otras estancias contiguas. Si la cocina es un espacio independiente al comedor, puede abrirse un pasaplatos o pueden instalarse puertas correderas de cristal para integrar los dos ambientes y permitir el paso de la luz. Habría que elegir un mobiliario de madera en tonos claros, frentes de armario en blanco, crudo o beige, o combinarlos con cristal; son trucos que contribuirán a que la cocina parezca más ligera y luminosa. Otras soluciones son colocar mesas de estructura ligera, taburetes que sustituyan sillas grandes y voluminosas y electrodomésticos de líneas rectas y discretas. Es necesario no recargar excesivamente el espacio, consiguiendo una cocina funcional pero ordenada. Si hay suficientes metros, una buena idea es colocar armarios sólo en la parte inferior de la zona de trabajo. Así la cocina parecerá más despejada. Colocar una isla de trabajo en el centro de la estancia permite distribuir cada una de las funciones de forma bien ordenada. Una buena iluminación artificial es imprescindible para poder trabajar con comodidad cuando el sol desaparece. Por ello es importante disponer de diversos puntos de luz en cada una de las zonas de la cocina: luz general en el techo y luz puntual en las áreas de cocción, trabajo y despensa.

Cuisines claires
Helle Küchen
COCINAS CLARAS
Bright Kitchens

Jaune intense
Intensives Gelb
INTENSIVE YELLOW
Amarillo intenso

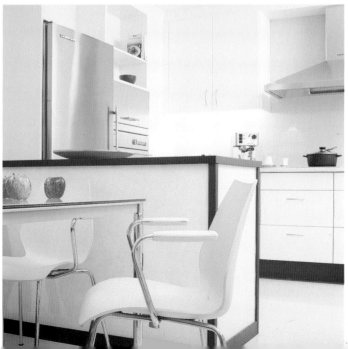

Blanc radieux
Strahlendes Weiß
RADIANT WHITE
Blanco radiante

373

Répartition
rationnelle
Rationelle Aufteilung
RATIONAL
DISTRIBUTION
Distribución racional

Photo © José Luis Hausmann

Des touches naturelles
Ein Hauch Natur
A TOUCH OF NATURE
Toques de naturaleza

Loft immaculé
Makelloses Loft
IMMACULATE LOFT
Loft inmaculado

Interiorism: **Sara Folch**

Photo © Jordi Miralles

Lumière continue
Kontinuierliches Licht
CONTINUOUS LIGHT
Luz continua

Architect: **Joan Bach**

Photo © Jordi Miralles

388

389

Nuances de lumière
Lichtnuancen
NUANCE OF LIGHT
Matices de luz

Architect: **Momo Brock**

DIRE

Table des
matières
Verzeichnis

CTORY

Directorio

DIRECTORY

VERZEICHNIS • TABLE DES MATIÈRES • DIRECTORIO

firms

Alessi *www.alessi.com*

Arclinea *www.arclinea.it*

Dornbracht *www.dornbracht.com*

Electrolux *www.elektrolux.com*

Elmar Cucine *www.elmarcucine.com*

Giemmegi Cucine *www.giemmegi.it*

Massimo Iosa Ghini (BD7) *www.iosaghini.it*

Philippe Starck *www.philippe-starck.com*

Snaidero *www.snaidero.com*

Toncelli *www.toncelli.it*

Zanussi *www.zanussi.com*

© Andrea Martiradonna

Photo credits:

Adriano Brusaferi: *p. 42*

Andrea Martiradonna: *p. 63*

Ake E. Son Lindman: *p. 53*

Carlos Domínguez: *p. 67, p. 85, p. 103, p. 107, p. 109, p. 121*

Concrete: *p. 109, p. 125*

Dennis Gilbert (View Pictures): *p. 77*

Eduardo Consuerga / Pablo Rojas: *p. 107, p. 111, p. 131*

Farshid Assassi: *p. 71*

Hannes Henz: *p. 75*

Hiroyuki Hirai: *p. 50*

Jan Baldwin (Narratives): *p. 79*

Jan Verlinde: *p. 55*

Jordi Miralles: *p. 8, p. 12, p. 13, p. 77, p. 79, p. 89*

José Luis Hausmann: *p. 83, p. 97, p. 112*

Juan Purcell: *p. 52*

Luis Cuartas: *p. 48, p. 73*

Mark Guard: *p. 81*

Michael Moran: *p. 59*

Mihail Moldeoveanu: *p. 89*

Montse Garriga: *p. 16, p. 24, p. 25, p. 26, p. 27, p. 28, p. 29, p. 30, p. 31, p. 33, p. 39, p. 41, p. 42, p. 43, p. 44, p. 46, p. 47, p. 65, p. 85*

Morel Marie Pierre: *p. 37*

Patrick Engquist: *p. 95*

Paul Ott: *p. 53*

Pep Escoda: *p. 91*

Pere Planells: *p. 8, p. 9, p. 11, p. 10, p. 17, p. 18, p. 19, p. 20, p. 21, p. 22, p. 23, p. 35, p. 36, p. 45, p. 49, p. 81, p. 97*

Peter Wenger: *p. 71*

Phillipe Saharoff: *p. 17*

Reto Guntli: *p. 87*

Ricardo Labougle: *p. 34, p. 35, p. 36, p. 37, p. 38, p. 45, p. 101*

Teisseire Laurent: *p. 10, p. 45*

Thomas Bruns: *p. 61*

Undine Pröhl: *p. 75*

Werner Huthmacher: *p. 129*

© Mateo Piazza

Other Designpocket titles by teNeues:

Bathroom Design 3-8238-4523-3

Berlin Apartments 3-8238-5596-4

Cafés & Restaurants 3-8238-5478-X

Cool Hotels 3-8238-5556-5

Country Hotels 3-8238-5574-3

Exhibition Design 3-8238-5548-4

Furniture/Möbel/Meubles/Mobile Design 3-8238-5575-1

Italian Interior Design 3-8238-5495-X

London Apartments 3-8238-5558-1

Los Angeles Houses 3-8238-5594-8

New York Apartments 3-8238-5557-3

Office Design 3-8238-5578-6

Paris Apartments 3-8238-5571-9

Product Design 3-8238-5597-2

Showrooms 3-8238-5496-8

Spa & Wellness Hotels 3-8238-5595-6

Staircases 3-8238-5572-7

Tokyo Houses 3-8238-5573-5

Each volume:

12.5 x 18.5 cm
400 pages
c. 400 color illustrations